The Assembly Celebrates

GATHERING THE COMMUNITY FOR WORSHIP

James Challancin

PAULIST PRESS
New York and Mahwah, N.J.

Library of Congress Cataloging-in-Publication Data

Challancin, James, 1941–
    The assembly celebrates : gathering the community for worship / by James Challancin.
        p.   cm.
    ISBN 0-8091-3096-3 : $5.95 (est.)
    1. Catholic Church—Liturgy.   2. Public worship.   I. Title.
BX1970.C46   1989
264'.02—dc20   89-8760
                                                                       CIP

Published by Paulist Press
997 Macarthur Boulevard
Mahwah, NJ 07430

Printed and bound in the
United States of America

Contents

Abbreviations

CSL   Constitution on the Sacred Liturgy

DCC   Dogmatic Constitution on the Church

EACW   Environment and Art in Catholic Worship*

GI   General Instruction of the Roman Missal

LMT   Liturgical Music Today*

MCW   Music in Catholic Worship*

RSV   Revised Standard Version of the New Testament

* Documents from the Bishops' Committee on the Liturgy issued with the authority of the National Conference of Catholic Bishops. The source of the other documents listed here are found in the text.

Introduction

Encouraging a sense of the worshiping community continues to be the number one concern for the new way we celebrate the liturgy. Gathering together is not incidental to our Sunday worship, but a very important feature of it. Yet, after more than twenty years, most of us average churchgoers are not aware of the significance which the assembly has. In particular, those of us who are Roman Catholics remain unfamiliar with the notion of a community gathering together for worship. Our Catholic training has too long emphasized only the Sunday obligation to attend mass. Church law still does. It is an obligation placed upon us which we may fulfill by slipping alone into one church or another where mass is being celebrated. Even though we actually assemble in church on Sunday, our coming together usually is not considered of any particular consequence.

But ever since the Second Vatican Council, church authorities have been insisting that mass is best celebrated by a gathering of people assembled around their bishop or, more commonly, around their ordained pastor. The council made this clear in its document, the *Constitution on the Sacred Liturgy* (CSL 41, 42). Later, when the sacramentary (the large altar book that contains the prayers for the mass) was revised as part of implementing the constitution, it was very definite about the priority given to "mass with a congregation." Before the revisions, the sacramentary had described the mass from the standpoint of the priest. It appeared to be entirely his activity; a congregation was not necessary.

The understanding of the church given to us by Vatican II is at the root of mass with a congregation, the new priority. There are two main ideas involved. First, the council saw the church as essentially a communion of persons united with the Lord and through him with one another. Second it saw how the community of the church becomes visibly present when the eucharist is celebrated by a gathering of the faithful. Put simply, we can see the communion which is the church when a particular group of its members gather together for the celebration of the eucharist. The church does not remain an abstract institution to which we belong, but through our celebration of the liturgy it becomes a tangible, definite communion in which we participate.

This is the significance of a local parish coming together on Sunday morning for the eucharistic celebration. It makes real the community of the church. As members of a parish we certainly must struggle for an actual, living union in our day to day dealings with each other. But when we gather together for the eucharist, it is a special moment for us to realize and to manifest the common union toward which we strive. And through that communion, the church itself is made present in the world.

Those of us with the responsibilities for preparing Sunday liturgy or for exercising a ministry in the actual celebration of it, indeed all of us who attend mass, must be aware of the great dignity that is ours on Sunday morning. We are entrusted with presenting the church to the world in a concrete, definite way. This we do in our celebration of the eucharist by becoming the gathered community of the faithful.

We find in the sacramentary that many parts of the liturgy have been redesigned to accomplish this purpose. We also find in the sacramentary an introductory chapter called the *General Instruction of the Roman Missal*. It describes each part of the mass showing the intent of the particular part and the spirit in which the part should be done. Priests accustomed to other kinds of liturgical documents are a little surprised when they read the general instruction. They expect to find only rules and directives for them to follow. But the instruction gives much more. The general instruction will be our main tool to help us understand what gathering together actually means and why it is now so important to the celebration. But our discussion is going to be practical too. Besides theory we need to know what parts of the liturgy are actually designed to bring about the gathered assembly and how we ought to be handling them. The general instruction does provide an understanding of what gathering together should mean. But it is much more concerned with the practical things, how to carry out the liturgy so that we become the gathered assembly, a real presence of the church in the world.

The first chapter will focus on those two principles from the Second Vatican Council that underlie the priority of gathering together: first, the church is essentially a community; second, our eucharistic celebration gives visible, tangible expression to that community of the church. Chapter 2 will look at the parts of the liturgy actually designed to build the unified assembly.

With the third chapter we will take up the important question of lay participation in the liturgy. It needs special attention because for so long we were not clear that lay persons were to have an active part in the celebration of the eucharist. The general instruction is emphatic that lay participation is a necessary constituent of the celebrating assembly. The chapter will conclude by looking at particular parts of the liturgy that have as their express purpose the incorporation of lay persons to the celebration.

Chapter 4 will consider lay, liturgical ministries from the perspective of how each of them can contribute to the building of the unified assembly. Many dimensions of these ministries, if done properly, can help us to see the bonds of faith that join us together. Liturgical ministries should help us to experience the community of the church as we celebrate.

"Gathering Together: All of Humanity, All of Creation," the conclusion, causes us to look beyond our immediate eucharistic assembly. Coming together is not the ultimate goal. No matter how effectively we may have carried out all the elements that give us an experience of camaraderie and communion, the gathering falls short if it does not look beyond itself. We are called into the eucharistic assembly so that we may be strengthened and prepared for our part in the greater gathering of God's people and, indeed, the whole of creation. Bringing God's unity and peace to our sisters and brothers and to the entire universe becomes the mission. For this there must be a dismissal from the assembly. We must be sent forth to our work of building God's kingdom.

1.

Gathering Together: A New Priority

Pestering the ushers to smile and to greet the people arriving for mass has become a regular duty for many parish liturgy committees. These committees are making some unsettling requests of the congregation as well. They attempt to summon members of the congregation out of their individual private prayer and encourage them to notice the other people who are present. For some of us it is a tense, uncomfortable moment when, at the beginning of mass, we are invited to introduce ourselves to the unknown persons standing with us in the same pew. But the big challenge is when we are asked to leave that home pew where we have traditionally sat since joining the parish. It is a little apart from the rest of the congregation, but it is not in the rear of the church nor is it behind a pillar. It does allow us to see the priest, answer the prayers, etc. Now all of sudden there seems to be some reason to move so that we can sit closer to other members of the parish.

Liturgy workshops and magazines from which the committees get their ideas talk about all these new demands as the need for hospitality, the need for creating an atmosphere of belonging in the congregation, the need for being with others. All of this is an indication of a new priority—"gathering together."

Many ordinary Catholics find it very bewildering. For so long simply attending mass on Sunday was the only priority. We know of it as the Sunday obligation. For many it is hard to appreciate why these new demands of gathering together are treated all so importantly. What difference does it make where one sits? Our duty, after all, is satisfied by getting to mass on time and by maintaining a prayerful, receptive attitude during the mass. Gathering together, sitting next to someone, extending hospitality—how do these things affect one's Sunday obligation?

It became particularly confusing a few years ago when some bishops began asking parishes to review their weekend mass schedules with an eye for a reduction in the number of masses celebrated. The shortage of clergy was one reason given. But it also was reasoned that fewer masses should help to insure an adequate number of people present for each of the celebrations. Scheduling many masses makes it convenient for people, but it also allows them to scatter their attendance so that some masses are left without enough people. But, again, it seems a strange trade-off to make the mass less available and the obligation more difficult to fulfill merely to increase the numbers attending one Sunday mass or the other.

Another dimension of previous learning also makes it hard for us to appreciate the new priority of gathering together. Holy cards so often depicted this dimension. They would show a priest standing reverently before the altar, holding up the host and chalice in a gesture of offering and adoration. What they suggested was that the priest's actions were the true actions of the eucharist, the ones upon which the prayerful attention of everyone else was to be focused. The duties of others involved in the celebration were not considered nearly as significant as those actions of the priest. From this perspective all the attention to the gathering of the people seems to be a distraction from what really counts in the mass.

How, then, to defend the concern being shown for the new priority when the role of the priest still demands respect, and the mass obligation continues to be the discipline of the church? The door is opened by the realization that these dimensions light up certain aspects of the eucharistic celebration, but do not encompass the whole reality. Celebrating the eucharist involves much more than the priest's actions and the people's obligation. We are being asked to balance our previous thinking with new insights so that we will come to a greater, more complete appreciation.

The priority of gathering together captures long neglected

dimensions of the eucharistic celebration. Two insights are especially involved. The first of these concerns the church itself. Increasingly it is appreciated as essentially a community, a united body of people. The second insight relates the church to the eucharistic celebration. It is the realization that the church as a community should be reflected in the way we celebrate the eucharist.

These ideas become prominent with the Second Vatican Council, and actually are drawn from the teaching of the council. They are not radically new ideas, but ideas that the bishops of the council found in the New Testament and the tradition of the church. It was the judgment of the bishops that these ideas could help to make the church and the celebration of the eucharist much more effective in the lives of the faithful. The first objective of Vatican II, after all, was: "To impart an ever increasing vigor to the daily Christian life of the faithful" (CSL 1).

OUR CHURCH, A COMMUNITY

"Parish family" is probably the phrase we have heard most often to express the notion of the church as a community. In a natural family, wife, husband and children are held together by mutual bonds of trust and love. Members of a parish share the common bond of faith. Like the bonds of a natural family, this bond draws us together so that, in some ways, we belong to each other like members of a family. This is what it means to recognize the church as a community. Because we are joined together by having the same faith in Jesus Christ, we are to form a united body of people, the community of the church.

To capture this reality the Second Vatican Council in its document, the *Dogmatic Constitution on the Church,* adopted the phrase "people of God." In the council's own words, God ". . . planned to assemble in the holy church all those who would believe in Christ" (DCC 2). God willed to save human beings "not merely as individuals without any mutual bonds, but by making them into a single people . . ." (DCC 9). Most of us grew up with a singular notion of the church as a way to our personal salvation. It tended to make our contact with the church very individual and private.

The council saw fit to expand our understanding so that we would also realize how we are the church, all of us drawn together and united by that bond of faith.

NEW TESTAMENT ROOTS

"People of God," which had become the characteristic insight of how the Second Vatican Council envisioned the church, comes originally from the New Testament (1 Pt 2:9–10). It sums up the great emphasis given in the New Testament to the church as a united body of people. In a rather idyllic way the Acts of the Apostles pictures the members of the early church living out their union through a common life:

> All who believed were together and had all things in common (Acts 2:44).

> Every day they devoted themselves to meeting together in the temple area and to breaking bread in their homes. They ate their meals with exultation and sincerity of heart . . . (Acts 2:46).

Besides these passages, expressions like "with one mind," "with one accord" and "all together" abound in Acts. They are used to describe the gatherings of the disciples. They indicate the close union which the Christian community is to have.

"Fellowship" words are St. Paul's way of urging the same thing. He frequently uses the word fellowship to describe how closely believers are united. Paul also makes clear that the bonds which bring them together are very deep, faith bonds. They are not just social contacts or merely shared interests. The bonds that hold the community together are "one Lord, one faith, one baptism, one God and Father of all" (Eph 4:5–6). As a result of such bonds, Paul considered it essential for a Christian community to work hard at being united. The members must recognize their unity and must strive to realize it in the way they behave toward one another.

In John's gospel, the new commandment is proclaimed, "Love one another, as I have loved you." This indicates the same close union which distinguishes the Christian community. The command is not put in singular, exclusive terms like "Love me, as I have loved you." Instead a disciple's love is to embrace the other disciples as well as the master. In fact, through love for one another their discipleship will become evident to the world. "This is how all will know that you are my disciples, if you have love for one another" (Jn 13:35).

They Actually Assembled

We often read these passages by ourselves and meditate on the community of love and faith we are to be as members of the church. But then we shy away from any real communal activity. The New Testament does not leave us in our reveries. It often shows us the disciples actually assembling to conduct the business of living in union with one another. In these accounts it is quite clear that the gatherings are very definite and concrete. The individuals present are mentioned frequently, and reference is often made to the place where the gathering is occurring. One phrase in particular is expressive of this concrete quality. It is, "all in one place together," a phrase regularly used to describe these assemblies. "All in one place together" significantly characterized the church at the moment of Pentecost (Acts 2:1). The same concrete meaning is carried by Paul's expression, "in church." He means the believers collected together in one place. Paul also mentions churches in the homes of particular Christians. It gives those churches a definite location. In the New Testament the community assembling was not an ideal but an actual occurrence which could be observed and experienced.

Assembling for Eucharist

One of the reasons for which the New Testament communities gathered was prayer. In Acts it is most often the reason for the community to be "all together." Paul is insistent that these prayer assemblies be times of harmonious accord (1 Cor 14:23–

40). His insistence will be especially urgent when the gathering is that of the eucharistic celebration.

The eucharist, the community's most central prayer, always was celebrated in an assembly. Jesus' command, "Do this in memory of me," was given to the disciples when they were assembled together. They continued to gather in one another's homes for its celebration. The eucharist was to be the corporate action of a community in fact assembled. It could not be otherwise.

Communion is the reason. According to Paul in 1 Corinthians 10 the deepest meaning of the celebration is a communion not only with the Lord but also with one another. The bread broken and the cup delivered is indeed a communion in the body and blood of Christ (1 Cor 10:16). But sharing in that communion brings a communion among the disciples as well: "Because the loaf of bread is one, we, though many, are one body, for we all partake of the one loaf" (1 Cor 10:17). As Paul's "fellowship" words indicate, along with John's new commandment, communion with the Lord causes the disciples to be united among themselves. Full communion with the Lord Jesus Christ includes living in fellowship with all of his followers. Paul is explicit that the same is true for the eucharist. The communion it brings is complete only when those celebrating realize that their bond with Christ is also a union with each other. Assembling for the celebration manifested the whole eucharistic communion, with the Lord and with one another. One could see in the actual gathering the communion of the disciples with one another, the effects of their communion with the Lord.

The eucharistic assembly, of course, would not be authentic unless those gathering were living a life of kindness, care, compassion and forgiveness for one another. But the actual assembling for eucharist was also important, for it gave symbolic expression to the communion. The New Testament example bearing this out is the community of Corinth. It is, unfortunately, a negative example. The divisions within the community were a cause of scandal. These divisions were obvious in the eucharistic celebration (1 Cor 11:17–34). The situation was so bad that Paul says it was not the

"Lord's supper" they were eating (1 Cor 11:20). They neither lived out the bonds of full eucharistic communion nor did they make the effort to give it symbolic expression when they celebrated. In Paul's estimation both were serious failures. The Corinthians were not a community at the eucharist but individuals and small factions. They all came to the same place for worship, but they did not truly assemble together. They did not join together into a gathering which would manifest the full eucharistic communion. One might say ironically that at least they were not hypocrites. They manifested in symbol what they actually were, a crowd of divided disciples.

Our priority today of gathering together can take an immediate lesson from its New Testament roots. The liturgical dimensions which presently engage us are important, necessary and worth the effort. Assembling together is the symbol which gives expression to the bonds of faith making us one. Sometimes, living out our faith bonds is emphasized as the only significant concern. Certainly, without the lived faith an authentic assembly cannot occur. But still the symbol of the assembly has its own power and force. In Paul's eyes both the lived faith and the assembly symbolic of it were essential. On the other hand, the lesson should also caution us against judging too quickly that no community exists when the persons present for the celebration are hesitant about the parts of the rite that build the assembly. Sometimes, more reticent habits of worship may hinder the expression while the faith bonds actually do exist.

The union of love among Christ's followers, according to John's gospel, manifested their discipleship to the world. In their communion with each other the church itself became visible as a united body of people. But Paul has an added emphasis. According to him the eucharistic assembly also imaged the church because it actually showed the disciples united. Paul gives considerable significance to this assembly, for it exhibits the disciples linked together through bonds of faith. The church, the community of believers, is present in the world not only through its members caring for one another, but also by visibly assembling for the eucharist.

THE NEXT GENERATION—STILL CONCERNED FOR COMMUNITY

Following the lead of the New Testament writers, the next generation of church leaders remained insistent about gathering together. They required the Christian community to assemble for prayer, for instruction and for the other common activities. Like St. Paul their underlying reason remained an urgency about the many faith bonds which joined the members together:

> But, with how much more right are they called brothers and considered such who have acknowledged one Father, God, who have drunk one spirit of holiness, who in fear and wonder have come forth from the one womb of their common ignorance to the one light of truth (Tertullian, *Apologetical Works*).

These early church leaders also showed a special concern about coming together for the eucharistic celebration. This assembly especially needed to manifest the unity of the members:

> No; at your meetings there must be one prayer, one supplication, one mind, one hope in love, in joy that is flawless, that is Jesus Christ, who stands supreme. Come together, all of you, as to one temple and one altar, to one Jesus Christ (St. Ignatius of Antioch, *Letter to the Magnesians*).

A special example is a very early manual of church teaching and tradition, the *Didache.* It contains a prayer for the eucharistic celebration which is reminiscent of 1 Corinthians 10:17 in the way it prays for the unity of the church:

> As this piece (of bread) was scattered over the hills and then brought together and made one, so let your church be brought together from the ends of the earth into your kingdom.

> Remember, Lord, your church . . . gather it together from the four winds. . . .

Sunday, Day of the Assembly

For this early generation of church leaders Sunday itself was not simply the day when one participated in the eucharist, as we tend to think of it. Instead, it was the day when all came together so that the eucharist could be celebrated:

> On that day which is named for the sun an assembly of everyone occurs in a single place. Those living in the city as well as those from the countryside come to the gathering (St. Justin, *Apologies*).

Amid all of this good theology about assembling, though, we already find scoldings, coaxing people to attend mass on Sunday. The seeming indifference to Sunday eucharist among some of the faithful which troubles us today has been with the church a long time. But the earnest persuasion given by these early church leaders was different than the warnings we receive. We usually are reminded about our individual obligation or the personal benefit of attending mass. The early church leaders, instead, admonished people to be attentive to the assembly because it manifested the church. Absenting oneself from the assembly diminished and scattered the church. It caused "the body of Christ to be short a member." There is the aspect of members attending for their own strengthening, but again the strengthening is not a matter of individual grace. Rather it is a benefit resulting from coming together. In expressing one's common faith by assembling with other believers there comes a mutual support and perseverance:

> Try to gather together more frequently to celebrate God's eucharist and to praise him. For when you meet with frequency, Satan's powers are overthrown and his destructiveness is undone by the unanimity of your faith (St. Ignatius of Antioch, *Letter to the Ephesians*).

Even during the persecutions, Christian communities remained adamant about gathering together for the Sunday eucharist. This was despite the dangers of being arrested, tortured and killed. In fact, taking part in common worship was considered by the state as proof of one's Christian convictions. These early martyrs could have had spiritual communion with the Lord anywhere or alone, as we can. They were even able to have sacramental communion separately, by themselves, for early customs of the church allowed the eucharist to be reserved in private homes. Mass was not celebrated daily but only on Sunday. Those wishing to receive communion more frequently were permitted to bring the blessed sacrament home with them and there take communion privately in their households.

Still, these early believers took the chance of regularly coming together to take part in the eucharistic assembly. A particular example is the African priest, Saturnius, and his community who were arrested and accused of assembling contrary to the edicts of the emperor Diocletian. They responded to the Roman proconsul that they had to celebrate the Sunday, the supper of the Lord. They could not be without the supper, and for this they needed to assemble.

Assembling at such risk may seem foolhardy to us. The reasons from our perspective would not seem to be worth the dangers. We are only beginning to realize the significance of celebrating the eucharist in the Christian community gathered together. The eucharistic piety in which we were formed valued mainly a personal communion with the Lord. This is the primary expectation most of us have for the sacrament. The early martyrs certainly valued personal communion, but also they saw an expression of their unity with one another as essential to the eucharist. It stemmed from the shared bonds of faith which joined them into one. They needed to assemble for the celebration so that their union of faith could be manifest. This they did even though they were threatened with death.

THE CHURCH REFLECTED IN EUCHARIST

The other insight underlying the priority of gathering together is the realization that how we celebrate the eucharist should reflect the nature of the church. It is also contained in these same sources of our tradition which led the Second Vatican Council to describe the church as a community. We have seen how the scandal of the Corinthian community was not only the failure to live their faith bonds, but also included the failure to celebrate the eucharist in a way that would show forth the unity which should have characterized them. The next generation of leaders likewise emphasized how the eucharistic assembly manifested the unity of its members. Since Paul's first letter to the Corinthians and the writings of the next generation are so insistent about the unity of the members being visible in the way they celebrate the eucharist, we come to realize that our eucharistic celebration should image the church in a visible, tangible way. This is the reason a group of members needs to gather for the celebration of the eucharist. Their coming together provides the visible evidence of the church as a united community.

Vatican II affirmed that the celebration of the eucharist shows forth the church. And it was very definite that the celebration of a gathered community, rather than the private mass of the priest, was the better manifestation of the church.

> The liturgy is thus the outstanding means by which the faithful can express in their lives, and manifest to others, the mystery of Christ and the real nature of the true church (CSL 2).

> . . . the church reveals itself most clearly when a full complement of God's holy people, united in prayer and in a common liturgical service (especially the eucharist), exercise a thorough and active participation . . . (CSL 41).

To this end the council declared the communal celebration of all the sacraments, but especially the eucharist, to be the preferred celebration (CSL 26, 27, 41, 42).

The church in its early tradition had been very aware of its members sharing one life, of its eucharist joining those members into one and of the celebration manifesting that union. It was such awareness which led the early church to insist upon a communal celebration. In the judgment of the Second Vatican Council there was a great reason for returning to the earlier tradition of liturgy celebrated in a communal way. It would help us to realize and show forth the church as a united community. This is the true dignity of the liturgical assembly. Whenever people come together to celebrate the eucharist their gathering images the church as a united body of people. It is the deep reason why gathering together deserves to be so prominent in our concern about how mass is celebrated.

GENERAL INSTRUCTION OF THE ROMAN MISSAL

Converting the pastoral wisdom of the council into an actual eucharistic celebration is the work of the *General Instruction of the Roman Missal*. It is imbued with concern for a liturgy that shows the church to be a united community. Expressions like "assembly," "gathered faithful," "people" and "community" are found readily in it. In fact, when the instruction was first published by itself, before the rest of the sacramentary, one of its articles, article 7, gave the impression that the whole significance of the mass was "the gathering of God's people."

The article was quickly criticized. What had happened to the great catechism explanations of the mass as holy sacrifice and the mystery of Jesus becoming really present under the forms of bread and wine? It did not appear at all correct to sum up the meaning of the mass as the assembly. In defense of article 7, however, the authors claimed that it represented the genuine tradition from 1 Corinthians. It could also be pointed out historically that, beginning in the fourth century, the prevailing name for the eucharistic celebration had been the "assembly" or the "communion." To eliminate any confusion the article was revised before it appeared in the sacramentary, but it continues to emphasize the importance of the gathered assembly.

Already we have looked at 1 Corinthians from the tradition of the church about assembling for the eucharist. And, indeed, this tradition underlies the whole of the instruction. But article 62 of the instruction stands out. In describing the role of the faithful it makes explicit references to aspects of the tradition. It uses St. Paul's reasoning from Ephesians 4 in warning the faithful to avoid any appearances of individualism or divisions when they gather for the eucharistic celebration. This must be the case because "they have one Father in heaven and therefore are all brothers and sisters to each other." Speaking positively, article 62 urges them to become "one body." It is an echo of those early church leaders who insisted so strongly that in the eucharistic assembly there must be one prayer, one mind and one altar.

Who Is the Celebrant of the Mass?

In a homey way, the concern of the general instruction for a communally celebrated liturgy gives us a new answer to the question we often ask on the way to church, "Who is celebrating mass today?" Buried in the usual answer we give is the presumption that the priest celebrates the mass and the rest of us attend. The new answer found in the instruction tumbles the presumption. It insists that the normal celebrant of the mass is all of us, the entire assembly.

The instruction gives this answer in many places. It explicitly states: "The celebration of Mass has the character of being the act of a community" (GI 14). Mass begins, according to the instruction, "after the people have assembled" (GI 25). Previously the mass was said to begin when the priest went to the altar. The architectural arrangements of church buildings are to be determined by the structures of "the people of God assembled at mass," and are to convey "the image of the gathered assembly" (GI 257). Finally article 7 in its revised form clearly states:

> At mass or the Lord's supper, the people of God are called together, with a priest presiding . . . to celebrate the memorial of the Lord or eucharistic sacrifice.

High Mass or Low Mass?

There is another homey effect which has come about because the general instruction places such an emphasis on the community celebration. We no longer distinguish between high masses and low masses. We used to make the distinction on whether an organist played, or whether six or two candles were lit. All of this is gone. It is a little humorous now to look back at how troubled we could get wondering if it were better to have one high mass offered or two low masses, or what difference six or two candles made.

Gone, too, are some other classifications of the mass, like the pontifical mass and the solemn mass. These distinctions depended on the rank which the celebrant held. A bishop or a monsignor of the proper level could celebrate a pontifical mass. Solemn mass needed a deacon and a subdeacon. Now the rank of the presider or additional ordained participants does not affect the form of the mass—people gathering does. In the sacramentary, "mass with a congregation" is designated the "basic" or "typical" way of celebrating (GI 78). It is placed first in the sacramentary and is arranged so that it can be used regularly. The role of the deacon is described so that he can be used in this or the concelebrated mass. But the basic structure of the celebration does not change because of his participation. "Concelebrated mass" and "mass without a congregation," the other classifications found in the sacramentary, are said to be variations of this "typical" form (GI 153, 210). Previously in church parlance the "typical" mass was a solemn form adapted so that a priest could celebrate it privately. He himself could carry it out assisted only by a server. People joining the celebration did not alter the form in any way.

CONCLUSION

We have grown somewhat accustomed to the communal view of the liturgy, but there is a sharp contrast between it and what had become the more prevalent notion. Before Vatican II the way we celebrated liturgy was influenced very much by the emphasis given to the priest celebrant and by the individual, personal way that the involvement of the rest of us was seen. We missed the importance of the assembly even when it did occur.

Just how sharp the contrast is can be measured by all the energy we still need to get the new priority of gathering together accepted. Our knowledge of how deeply gathering together is rooted in the tradition of the church should encourage us. The gathered assembly is not simply the relevant, pastoral ploy of the moment, but the wisdom of the church gained from its long experience. It also helps to remember that the present concern comes from the pastoral decisions of the Second Vatican Council. In its judgment the renewal of the liturgy and of the church itself depends very much on the new emphasis being given to gathering together.

Finally, the new priority of gathering together enjoys the full authority of the church. The official altar book to be used is the present sacramentary with its emphasis on gathering the community.

2.

Building
the Unified Assembly

"Gathering together" means celebrating the eucharist in such a way that we give expression to the church as a community. It means actually collecting ourselves in one, visible, tangible place. But once we are together, more is expected than physical coexistence. Here the priority becomes more difficult to describe. It can easily appear as though the primary purpose of coming together is to experience warm, good feelings, those belonging to close, human friendship. Such a direction can lead to some unrealistic demands for an intimacy more appropriate to our natural families or our personal companions.

According to Vatican II, in fact, as we have seen, the whole tradition of the church gathering together is founded upon a bond of faith rather than personal affections. On the other hand, gathering together is not a cold recitation of the creed in unison either. This is clear from St. John's "See how they love one another," and from the recounting in Acts how the disciples "partook of food with glad and generous hearts." Somewhere between an excessive enthusiasm for community and a demonstration of faith without feelings lies "gathering together."

What gathering together should mean can be discovered by studying the *General Instruction of the Roman Missal*. It contains the understanding of gathering together intended by the Second Vatican Council. But we do not find in the general instruction a theoretical discussion about the priority. Instead it gives us definite, concrete ways to form a unified assembly. It incorporates elements of emotions and feelings so that the bond of faith becomes a tangible experience for us and not just a conviction existing only in our minds. But it avoids extremes as well, so that we experience the bonds of faith and not just good feelings of camaraderie. Gathered together in an experience of faith unity, as intended by the general instruction, we become a unified assembly. Through that assembly, expression is given to the church as a community of faith and love.

Like the general instruction itself this chapter will not be a theoretical discussion about gathering together. Instead it will discuss the concrete elements provided by the general instruction to bring about the gathering. It will give us many insights about how we ought to celebrate the eucharist. But besides these insights, it will boost our confidence. We will come to appreciate that gathering together is not some innovative idea or private notion but honestly what the church wants when we celebrate mass.

THINGS DONE TOGETHER

Among the primary means which the general instruction gives us to build the unified assembly are those things we do together. In particular the acclamations and responses are said to be important for a communal involvement of all present (GI 15). Some examples of acclamations are those which occur as part of the eucharistic prayer: the Holy, holy, the memorial acclamation and the great Amen. The psalm response after the first reading would also be an example of a communal response, as the name indicates.

So often we do these things as though simply getting the words said were enough. Maybe it goes back to when all the acclamations and responses were done by the choir. Or, if there were no choir, then the organist provided them in one manner or another. A single voice rendering the acclamations and responses could easily give the impression that simply singing (or saying) the words was adequate.

The real intent of the acclamations and responses is to provide us with common words which we can sing or say together.

Done commonly, the acclamations and responses create the experience of a unified assembly. But we need to be conscious that we are doing them together and not as separate, lonely voices. We need to be aware of each other, listening to each other, as we speak or sing the same words. Done in this way the acclamations and responses help to break down the feelings that many of us have of being in the same place with others of the faithful, but there worshiping individually and privately. We simply have not performed acclamations and responses properly if we only speak them ourselves, even if we voice them as expressive of our inner, personal prayer. There also needs to be an awareness of the other faithful saying or singing them along with us. Then these acclamations and responses become what they are intended to be, an expression of that bond of faith which joins us all together.

For this reason we should sing most of the acclamations and responses. Singing is the way of praying together. When we sing, the music provides rhythm and melody which help to keep us together as the spoken word cannot. Just think of some of the recited Our Fathers you have heard. They usually end with individuals crossing the finish line in first, second or third place. Rhythm and melody hold us together.

They also weave our many voices into one. Rhythm and melody blend together the trained and untrained, the off-key, the male and female, the young and the old. Sung acclamations and responses have a better chance to create an awareness of our unity in faith as we celebrate the eucharist.

There is also that intangible, unifying quality about music. We feel it when we are just singing for the fun of it and find ourselves putting an arm around the person next to us. We know it too when we sing the national anthem or our school or sorority song. We forget ourselves and become bonded to the people with whom we share values and sentiments.

Unfortunately most of us do not experience this quality of music in our sung acclamations and responses. But the potential is there. If they do not have this unifying quality it may be because they still are not familiar to us and still are not a shared experience for us. We may need to settle for a few good ones and not change them too frequently, rather than a changing variety to which we remain strangers. The hope that our singing at mass will eventually have this intangible, unifying quality is certainly worth the effort.

Besides acclamations and responses the general instruction designates certain parts of the rite to be done by the whole gathering. These are the penitential rite, the profession of faith, the general intercessions and the Lord's prayer (GI 16). Like acclamations and responses these parts also provide common words to help us appreciate being part of the assembly. Finally the instruction sees common body postures—standing, sitting and kneeling—as demonstrating the assembly gathered into one (GI 62, 21). But, of course, besides doing them in unison, we also need to be aware that they express our faith unity.

The point deserves some instruction. Now oftentimes our only motivation for wanting to know the proper postures is so that we can be correct, and not be embarrassed by standing or sitting at the wrong times. Expressing our faith unity is a much richer motivation. The sacramentary gives the basic directives about when to stand, sit, kneel, etc. On occasion, before mass, these postures could be reviewed with the whole assembly, but from the perspective of common actions expressing our bonds of unity. It should not be done merely as a matter of keeping the celebration tidy.

DIALOGUES BETWEEN THE CELEBRANT AND CONGREGATION

The dialogues between the celebrant and the congregation deserve special attention. They, too, are identified as outward signs of the celebration's communal nature (GI 14). The instruction recognizes how the dialogues are means to a greater communion between priest and people (GI 14). Certainly, any level of communion achieved within the liturgical gathering enhances the experience of a unified community. But in addition, highlighting the communion of the people with the priest has a special significance. It goes back to the lesson taught us by the holy card images in which the eucharist appeared to be entirely the work of the priest. The people being brought into dialogue with the priest shows their actions, along with his, to be important for the celebration. Or better, to use the terminology of the general instruction, the eucharist is "normally" celebrated communally rather than by one particular individual alone. The priest's action remains central but ideally it draws the other faithful together into the celebration. By placing the priest's essential role into dialogue with the community a broader perspective is being offered by the general instruction to persons who may still consider what the priest does "up there in the sanctuary" as the only actions "that count."

A place where this feature has particular application is in determining what parts of the mass we should sing. Those parts to be sung by the presider with the congregation responding or by the presider and people together really should be given preference (GI 19). This preference is not mentioned very often. As a result the entrance dialogue, the exchange that occurs at the beginning of mass, is seldom considered a part to be sung. Music is provided for it in the sacramentary. Another instance would be the dialogue introducing the eucharistic prayer. It should be sung frequently as it once was—for it joins the people to the priest.

One obvious thing cannot be overlooked. As dialogues, these parts of the rite are persons speaking to each other. They are not simply reciting words into the air for God's benefit, an impression so often given by both presiders and congregations. These dialogues need to be done with an awareness that we are speaking to another. Much depends upon the presider. His eye contact with the congregation and the expressiveness with which he speaks the ritual phrases of the dialogue are quite important.

But all of us in the congregation as well need to speak our words with purpose and meaning as we respond. A congregation clearly speaking with conviction makes a difference to itself and to the presider. The faith of both is strengthened. When the words spoken in the exchange have the qualities of true dialogue, they forcefully bring about a unified assembly. Unifying faith is plainly seen and can be tangibly felt.

INTRODUCTORY RITES

Three major changes were made by the general instruction in the way mass was to be celebrated. These are the introductory rites, the preparation of the gifts and the communion rite. All three contain elements to build the unified assembly.

The introductory rites carry a special burden. Before coming to mass we have all been about our own separate activities. We have come with diverse joys, cares and worries. Most of us have not seen each other since the previous Sunday. Now that we are together again, the introductory rites have the special importance of beginning the work to unite us for this celebration.

A stated purpose for the introductory rites is "that the faithful coming together take on the form of a community" (GI 24). The entrance song, greeting to the congregation and the opening prayer are especially important in bringing about this purpose. The song is to "intensify the unity of the gathered people" (GI 25). The greeting is "to the assembled community," and expresses "the mystery of the gathered church" (GI 28). In the opening prayer the people are to be invited to pray together with the priest (GI 32).

Entrance Song

The entrance song can be very effective in unifying the assembly because, as we have already mentioned, it has a bonding power. Spirited songs that can be sung easily especially spark a solidarity within a group. Those school songs, team "fight" songs, and the hymns of sororities and fraternities are always spirited ones. Invariably the public demonstrations we witness, be they for pro-life, peace, disarmament or a minority cause, all make use of spirited songs to unify their ranks. Bonded together this way, the individual members are encouraged to remain firm in their purposes. Music of similar strength is needed for the entrance song.

In popular discussions we are beginning to hear "gathering song" rather than the official name "entrance song," given in the general instruction. The new name better indicates the song's purpose of intensifying the unity among us as we gather to celebrate the eucharist. Reflecting the new, popular designation is the practice sometimes found of the presider and the other ministers making their entry during instrumental music. Only when they have reached their places in the assembly does the gathering song begin. Although the general instruction lists accompanying the procession among the purposes of the song, still the new practice may at times be preferred. With gathering together a main priority the unifying purpose of the song is the one properly emphasized.

More commonly, the musicians are showing an appreciation of the unifying purpose by allowing the song to continue even after the presider has reached the chair. They do not end it abruptly as is often the case when the song is simply understood to accompany the entrance of the priest. There is another bit of evidence that the unifying purpose is increasingly being appreciated. Far less frequently is the entrance song being announced as greeting the celebrant. During the month of May it was always a little embarrassing for the male presider to enter in procession after the announcement had been made, "Let us greet our celebrant with 'Hail, Holy Queen.'"

Greeting of the Congregation

One of the deep reasons for the assembly occurring is symbolized by the greeting of the congregation. In the Old Testament, God, speaking to the Israelites, summoning them together, formed the people of God. The options we have for greetings are adapted passages from scripture (Rom 1:7; 2 Cor 13:14). In the ritual moment they are God speaking to us, calling us together into a new people. It is the same word of God, the same call. God is constant. Through the greeting of the congregation our immediate eucharistic assembly is summoned to respond to God's insistent gathering of a people.

Appreciating the greeting of the congregation as God calling a new people together gives us some important insights about the assembly. First, like all of salvation, the gathering is at God's initiative. The Israelites did not assemble into a people of their own accord, but in response to God's plan for them. So the eucharistic gathering is not simply the like-minded coming together for sharing and mutual support. Assembled at God's initiative the eucharistic gathering is with whomever God has called. There are not the limitations there might be if the gathering were at our design and depended upon our good will. If done according to our intentions alone, the gathering easily falls short, including only friends, prayer-partners and the like, rather than all who assemble.

Second, the particular gathering in which we actually assemble is the one to which God speaks and the one summoned to be God's people. The Old Testament does not record an abstract, generic call to the Israelites. Instead in the book of Exodus they are assembled in a very definite place, at Mount Sinai, and there God spoke to them (Ex 19). In a similar way our individual eucharistic assemblies provide definite places where God may speak to us (cf. GI 9, 33). Thus the actual eucharistic assembly in which we participate has some of the same awesomeness as did the gathering at Sinai. The scriptural greetings provided carry that weighty implication. Chatty greetings like "good morning" do not. "At mass . . . the people of God are called together . . ." (GI 7).

There is a third insight. The Israelites were given their identity as the people of God in the particular assembly at Sinai, but the designation also had a universal meaning. It extended to the entire nation as well. People of God also carries a universal dimension for us. Besides referring to the specific gatherings of our eucharistic assemblies, the whole church throughout the world is God's people. As a matter of fact, the universal meaning is the only one to be found in the documents of the Second Vatican Council. At the time of the council, twenty years ago, it was the more common meaning.

In the general instruction, though, people of God usually refers to the particular gathering (GI 7, 9, 33, 62, 74, 259). This would be expected since the instruction governs celebrations of the eucharist. These always occur in specific, gathered assemblies. But the general instruction also makes references to the universal meaning (GI 1, 10, 257). We cannot forget that the eucharist unites us not only with the persons who have gathered, but also with the whole church throughout the world. Again, the greeting of the congregation needs the substance of scripture in order to indicate the full communion of God's people. It cannot simply evoke the friendly companionship of our immediate gathering.

The general instruction in describing the greeting speaks of another reason underlying the assembly's coming together. It describes the greeting as a moment when the Lord's presence is declared to the community (GI 28). Christ promised to remain with us; his presence is a bond of unity for us. Remember Paul had included "one Lord" in the reasons for Christians to be unified in their living together (Eph 4:5, cf. 1 Cor 12:5). Also in Ephesians, Paul identifies Jesus as the "capstone," the one who fits together the whole structure of God's household (Eph 2:20–21). In the renewal of Vatican II Jesus as the life and unity of the church is a central teaching. Calling attention to Christ's presence, as the greeting does, helps us to realize why we are to assemble into a community (GI 24). All of the options provided make mention of Christ's presence including the one reserved for the bishop, "Peace be with you." Peace is part of Christ's farewell, part of his abiding presence to his disciples (Jn 14:27).

The brief remarks which the presider or other minister may give introducing the mass of the day are another moment when our gathering together can be nourished. These remarks were found to be very effective in moving persons away from a strictly individual experience of mass. In a study of parish worship done a few years ago, it was found that if these remarks were omitted, then usually there would be poor rapport between the presider and the congregation, people participated less, and the community spirit suffered. While these introductory remarks are not intended to be casual like "good morning," as is so often heard, still an element of welcome can be present as the presider (or other appropriate minister) sets the tone for the particular celebration.

Opening Prayer

The third element of the introductory rites that furthers the purpose of gathering together is the opening prayer. It is one of those dialogues between the congregation and presider which are particularly significant for a communal awareness. The dialogue structure requires that our presiders appreciate the importance of the words, "Let us pray," as an invitation to all of us. We, in turn, must realize that we are responding to an invitation when we enter into the silent part of the prayer and when we answer "Amen." Giving an invitation or responding to it, calls for attentiveness and enthusiasm. An absent-minded, haphazard "Amen" is not the kind of response appreciated when one gives an invitation. Like the prayer of the presider our "Amen" needs to be strong and vigorous.

"Collect" is an alternate name for the opening prayer (GI 32). It indicates how a purpose of the prayer is to gather the many intentions of all the faithful into one united supplication before God. The time of silence after the "Let us pray" allows for this to occur. In the silence each of us is able to call to mind our particular needs and longings. Then there is actually something to be collected. Without the silence there is no time for us to become aware of our intentions and there is nothing to be joined into one unified prayer. The prayer is not a "collect" under those circumstances and thus does not function so well at building up our gathered assembly.

The silence of the opening prayer has another purpose which also reflects how the prayer helps to unite the assembly. The other purpose which the general instructions gives is so that the people can come to realize they are in God's presence (GI 32). God's presence is a foundation for our unity because it makes us aware of our common creaturehood, our common needs and our common destiny. It also makes us aware of God's will that there be harmony and peace among all humanity.

Other Helps

Besides words there are other helps to communicate the unifying power of the introductory rites. One of them is the gesture of outstretched arms made by the presider while speaking the words of greeting (GI 86). In it the presider with arms extended to the congregation becomes a symbol of God's embrace, an embrace which makes us one. The open-armed gesture when friends are found at the door provides the appropriate model. It is a body movement that communicates welcome because bonds of friendship exist. It also communicates delight because these bonds will be enjoyed and strengthened in this visit. The gesture, though, is not a casual one, offered to buddies. It needs a touch of solemnity so that it can communicate the welcome and delight of friendship with God.

The other help is the presider's visual presence to the community. Being able to see the presider supplies a focal point not only for our eyes but also for our attention. It helps to hold us to our common purpose rather than wandering into private reverie. Since the general instruction sends the presider to the chair upon arrival, the chair should be located so that a visual presence is possible. The altar or some other object should not pose a physical barrier obscuring the presider from the congregation. If the chair is poorly situated, then during the more active moments of leadership in the celebration, the presider should stand away from the chair, closer to the people, in order to be adequately visible to them. For the same reason servers should not flank the presider. They should be inconspicuously located, coming forward only when needed.

In recent experience there has been a rediscovery of how attention to the arrival of the participants can greatly enhance the effectiveness of the introductory rites, creating a communal awareness for us. Unfortunately the general instruction only attends to the arrival of the presider and some few of the other ministers. Members of the congregation are left to make their own way. On the positive side the general instruction does not give an emphasis to the entrance procession and does not intend it to be a primary part of the introductory rites (cf. MCW 44). The introductory rites, after all, are about all of us coming together, not just the entrance of the presider and ministers. Still the presider and ministers moving through the congregation in procession can give a sense of the whole community coming together. For this reason it should be done with care, dignity and ceremony. It should not be a casual amble to the presider's chair.

But an alternate has been suggested in which the presider and ministers would quietly take their places without ceremony, much like other members of the community do. At the appropriate time the presider would stand, step forward into a prominent place and assemble the community by calling it to prayer. The gathering song would occur after the presider had assembled the congregation. The similar arrival of all participants centers the attention on the total gathering. In this way the variation—done on occasion—could help to create that communal awareness, the primary purpose of the introductory rites.

The introductory rites considered so exclusively from the perspective of forming the assembly may seem to be an exaggeration. This could be our impression especially since another purpose is also given in the general instruction, namely that of preparing for the liturgy of the word and the liturgy of the eucharist (GI 24). But the emphasis can be defended because the way in which the introductory rites prepare for those two major parts of the mass is by gathering us into a community. We arrive for the celebration from many different circumstances of life. Moving us from this diversity into an awareness of our mutual bonds prepares us to hear the word and to celebrate the eucharist. At Sinai God first gathered the people together, then spoke to them. For us, we must be assembled in order to hear God's word. The privileged reading of the scriptures, according to the *Constitution on the Sacred Liturgy*, occurs in the gathering of the church (#7). Brought to a more intense unity by hearing God's word together, we are moved to celebrate the eucharist. The two stated purposes of the introductory rites are really one purpose, to prepare us for the word and eucharist by forming us into a unified assembly.

PREPARATION OF THE GIFTS

The preparation of the gifts, the second part of the mass rite significantly changed, has been redesigned so that it too is a communal activity. The prayers and actions in this part of the mass had been entirely those of the presider assisted only by the servers. The new arrangement adds the gifts procession in which representatives of the congregation bring the bread and wine to the altar and present them to the presider. This exchange is really intended to be the focus of the preparation although many of the prayers and activities of the presider remain (GI 49, 101; cf. MCW 46). With the central actions shared by members of the congregation, the preparation of the gifts clearly becomes an activity of the whole assembly.

But to realize the communal nature, presiders in particular must appreciate the new focus, for they were the ones who were previously occupied with the many detailed gestures. What remains of these gestures is not the center of attention. Styles of priestly fussiness and liturgical bustle, especially, should be avoided. Encouraging representatives of the congregation to bring up the gifts and accepting them with graciousness and warmth now ought to be the first concerns of the presider.

The exchange of gifts needs to be given adequate time as well, and should be done in a place clearly visible to everyone so that its significance is appreciated. When a song is done at this time it properly should celebrate the communal aspects of the exchange. The song need not speak of bread and wine or of offering as we sometimes think it must. Actually songs which speak generally of praise and joy are better (MCW 71).

Before moving on, there is one practice in bringing up the gifts which should be discouraged. Very often among the gifts to be presented is a separate paten with only the priest's host on it. It speaks of a separation rather than unity, and violates that communal dimension which the preparation of the gifts is redesigned to contain. It would be much better to follow the recommendation of the general instruction and use one paten large enough to hold all the bread needed for the entire assembly (GI 293). There is nothing in the general instruction which suggests that the presider's host should be kept separate. Rather it presumes one paten with all of the hosts on it. This practice would give the better symbol to encourage the unified assembly.

A case also can be made for the inclusion of the chalice as part of the gifts procession. Presently it is to be brought directly to the altar along with the corporal, purificator, etc., as part of the altar preparations. The chalice brought to the altar like that, in a different manner than the paten, has a long tradition. But the tradition assigns no particular meaning why the chalice should be reserved in such a way. The chalice excluded from the gifts procession could intimate some sort of clerical exclusivity. Included, it would reinforce the preparation of the gifts as the activity of the whole assembly.

Communion, the third part of the mass rite to be greatly altered, is the culminating moment in which the Lord brings together a new people of God. It has always been such a moment. But the rite for communion had become tangled and gave us little appreciation of our becoming a people united in Christ. There were actually two separate sets of prayers leading to communion, one for the priest, another for anyone else who wanted to receive—few others did. Practically, the experience was of separate communions. It reinforced the notion that communion amounted to individuals being united with the Lord alone through their reception of the blessed sacrament. It gave no awareness of what we have seen from the New Testament and from those other later writings where communion with the Lord is complete only when it leads us to be united among ourselves.

The changes have restored one whole communion rite. Very significantly there is a single introduction providing one of those dialogue moments between the priest and congregation. The rite now is much more symbolic of a communion with the Lord which gathers us into one. The general instruction is very explicit. When it describes the role of the congregation, it urges us to become one body especially by "sharing together in the Lord's table" (GI 62).

The immediate preparations for communion likewise have been redesigned to help bring about an experience of the assembly coming together. The Lord's prayer, the rite of peace and the breaking of the bread have all been redirected. Now their purpose is clearly to help us become one with all the others who have gathered.

The Lord's Prayer

With the changes, the Lord's prayer is one to be said by all. In the former directives it was a prayer said by the priest alone. Now all of us voice the petition for the coming of the kingdom, a kingdom of "peace and unity" (cf. prayer from the rite of peace). We all pledge ourselves, out loud, to forgiveness and reconciliation, qualities without which we are unable to live at one with other people. Each of us declares that the Father in heaven is indeed "Our Father." It goes without saying that when the Lord's prayer is sung the music should allow for everyone to participate. It is not the place for a solo. (The Lord's prayer is seldom done as a solo in regular parish masses, but often it is done that way at weddings and funerals. It is as inappropriate in those occasions as it is at the regular masses.)

Rite of Peace

The rite of peace, before the changes occurred, was done only during solemn high mass and did not stand out as something especially significant in the ceremonies, although it did hold a certain fascination. Moms liked to tell their youngsters about it and alerted them to watch for it. Structurally, it was mostly a clerical thing, beginning with the celebrant and being passed down through the ranks of the clergy to the servers. It stopped there and was not offered to the congregation.

Now, it has been restored as a gesture for the entire gathered assembly. All of us are to exchange a sign of peace with those standing nearby. The prayer which precedes the invitation to offer one another a sign of peace prays that the peace and unity of the Lord's kingdom will begin to be found among us. It leaves little doubt that the intent of the rite is to help us realize the unified assembly.

The usual gestures for the sign of peace, a handshake or an embrace, effectively convey what we are about in this part of the preparation for communion. While there is some freedom about the words used in the exchange of peace, the reality for which we ask is not conveyed by expressions of pleasant good wishes or by merely voicing our bonds of friendship and love. "Have a nice day" or "I love you, dear" are not adequate expressions for the rite of peace. As the prayer of the rite indicates, it is the special peace of Christ for which we ask, his parting gift to the church. The bonds which it celebrates are those of faith uniting us into Christ's body. Our human bonds of love and friendship can help us to understand the peace of Christ, but ultimately his peace is greater than these human attachments.

The same rationale makes it clear that we should never avoid the sign of peace simply because we find ourselves among strangers. We may not enjoy bonds of friendship with them, but we still share bonds of faith, and these are the deepest motivations we have to offer a sign of peace.

Hypocrisy is another motive for some of us to keep from the rite. Knowing our own insincerity or observing it in others, we hold back from the sign of peace. Rarely should this happen. No doubt we must take very seriously Matthew 5:23–25, "If you . . . recall that your brother has anything against you . . ." We must come to the rite with lives marked by the hard work of forgiveness and love. But being human there are always divisions among us and our desires for peace are never without flaw. People exchanging the sign can always appear to be hypocritical. The unity and peace we have is never perfect or even adequate.

The rite however is a prophetic gesture. Prophetic gestures proclaim the small beginnings of God's grace within us and encourage us to look ahead for greater fulfillment. True, we pray for "peace in our day" (prayer following the Lord's prayer) but, at last, we look ahead and petition for the "peace and unity" of the kingdom which is to come (prayer from the rite of peace).

Breaking of the Bread

The mention of the "breaking of the bread" usually brings blank stares to people's faces. Very few of us recognize that part of the mass, the most immediate preparation for communion. Yet, the general instruction is very definite and forceful about it:

> The eucharistic bread should be made in such a way that in a mass with a congregation the priest is able actually to break the host into parts and distribute them to at least some of the faithful (GI 283).

The importance of this reform has not yet been grasped. It remains enough to feel for the raised line on the reverse side of the large host, then crack the host along that line into two equal portions.

But even the second portion is not usually offered to anyone else, but is consumed by the priest himself. Also at concelebrated masses a seeming rubric often persists that each priest must take both pieces of a large broken host. Even concelebrants do not necessarily share one bread among themselves. For the rest of us it is always small hosts.

The symbol of bread broken and shared is not appreciated even though, as the instruction observes, it was done by Christ at the last supper and named the whole eucharistic celebration since apostolic times (GI 56c). Repeatedly the general instruction emphasizes the sign of unity which the breaking of the bread is to be (GI 48, 56c, 283). Nothing shows better the assembly being drawn together through its celebration of the eucharist than does this gesture of bread being shared. Because it is the "one bread of life," Christ himself, nothing is more effective in causing us to become the "one body" (GI 56c).

But some progress has been made. There are church supply companies who now offer a large host about eight to ten inches in diameter. These can be broken and shared with at least some of the congregation. On weekdays a host like that is often large enough to provide communion for everyone present. There are also parishes that bake their own loaves using an approved recipe. Then many can share from the one loaf.

But using small, individual hosts remains the prevalent practice. Despite the practicality, the general instruction is not enthusiastic about small hosts. It merely permits them, saying that if you must, they are not forbidden (GI 283). Using small, individual hosts simply destroys the symbol of bread broken and shared.

Another devastating practice regularly occurring is communion from hosts reserved in the tabernacle. Again the instruction is very firm and emphatic:

> It is most desirable that the faithful receive the Lord's body from hosts consecrated at the same mass . . . (GI 56h).

But the habit is tenacious. Church authority has been discouraging it since the sixteenth century.

As to the actual breaking of the bread, it should be done with dignified, wholesome gestures, and should be visible to the whole congregation. It should not be lost in the midst of other activities like the eucharistic ministers approaching the altar. That should have already occurred. (The eucharistic ministers best approach the altar after the great Amen. The presider should wait for them before beginning the "Lord's prayer." Or, the ministers may approach while the sign of peace is being exchanged.) If necessary, special ministers of the eucharist may help with the breaking so that it is done effectively but does not take overly long. The "Lamb of God" may be extended beyond its usual three invocations to accompany the whole breaking of the bread (GI 56e). Adequate care should be taken so that tiny particles are not lost, but no excessive fastidiousness is required.

Moment of Communion

The moment of communion itself stands ahead of everything else in building up the unified assembly. We have not always been aware of this reality because our personal communion with the Lord has sometimes seemed to be more important. Still it is a traditional teaching of the church that "the first fruit of the eucharist is the unity of the body of Christ" (MCW 48). It looks back to St. Paul: "Because the loaf of bread is one, we, though many, are one body, for we all partake of the one loaf" (1 Cor 10:17).

Certainly communion in the body of Christ is first the work of the Lord. But there is a natural symbolism involved to which St. Paul is referring (cf. GI 283). It is that of sharing food. The communion moment has always been eating and drinking the body and blood of the Lord.

The natural symbolism of sharing food, eating a meal together, speaks strongly of life shared together. Holiday time always finds us desiring to be around the table with our family and friends where we can celebrate all the memories and bonds that unite us. Missing holiday meals with the family has its way of making us strangers. The people with whom we eat are the people to whom we belong. Regrettably one of the things about our twentieth century lifestyle is its schedules filled with activities that leave no time for family members to eat together. This plays its part in weakening family ties.

The symbolism of the eucharist as food shared, a meal eaten together, is very prominent in the general instruction. It speaks of the "force and meaning" in "one bread being distributed among members of one family" (GI 283). Often the general instruction refers to the celebration as the "Lord's supper" (GI 2, 3, 281) and to the altar as the "Lord's table" (GI 8, 49, 62, 259). It also speaks of the eucharist as the paschal meal and the eucharistic banquet (GI 48, 56, 240, 241, 268).

To Catholic ears the "Lord's supper" may sound Protestant. But once more St. Paul is the source. It is his language. In 1 Corinthians 10:21 he refers to "the table of the Lord," and in 11:20 actually to "the Lord's supper." Speaking of the eucharist as a paschal meal and as a banquet also is from the New Testament (Mt 26:17, 29; Mk 14:12, 25; Lk 22:8, 15–18). There are other dimensions to the eucharistic celebration, but the meal symbol is a prominent one and is not a new notion. It is the scriptural tradition. It all begins with the first three gospels recording how the eucharist was instituted during a meal, the last supper (cf. GI 48).

Thus the general instruction has strong authority behind it when it stresses the symbol of the eucharist as a meal. With such an emphasis we can appreciate how eating and drinking the body and blood of the Lord is an effective symbol to unite us with each other as well as with the Lord.

On the practical side of the meal symbol, the general instruction recommends that the bread used actually have the appearance of food (GI 283). This is another reason why some parishes bake their own. It provides a bread that looks somewhat more like bread as we know it. A while ago some restrictions were placed on the ingredients which may be used in making the bread, but it is still quite possible to bake one's own.

Communion Under Both Kinds

Being able to drink from the cup as well as to receive the consecrated bread has a special significance for restoring the meal symbol of the eucharist. The U.S. bishops, when they introduced communion under both kinds, made this one of the reasons to encourage drinking from the cup. Food and drink together are the staple elements which signify a meal for us. Thus, adding the cup gives a better expression to the meal symbol of the eucharist. The enhanced meal symbol, in turn, is more effective in joining us together. In the words of the fourth eucharistic prayer we pray, "Gather all who share this one bread *and one cup* into the one body of Christ."

Wine at the banquet assures festivity and communion among the guests. It may seem a little out of place, but the hearty camaraderie which develops when table partners share a little wine should be recalled as part of the communion symbol. It is part of what wine does. If we need a little encouragement, the psalmist does sing about wine cheering our hearts (Ps 104:15). Recalling the natural camaraderie of wine drunk together as we drink from the communion cup adds its effectiveness to the symbolic gesture drawing us together into the one united people.

Directives from the U.S. bishops have been consistent and careful that taking the precious blood would be done in such a way so as to give a strong symbol of the communion and unity it brings. They have resisted the use of small, individual communion cups, a custom in some Protestant churches. They have also discouraged intinction, i.e., dipping the host into the cup. Sharing a common cup and actually drinking from it is the better symbol of unity. These discouraged practices would not be so inappropriate if communion under both kinds were simply a better symbol of communion with the Lord. But under both kinds it also has a special effectiveness in symbolizing our communion with one another.

The chalice really ought to be used as one of the common communion cups. Now it is usually reserved for the priest and sometimes the assistant eucharistic ministers. But reserved that way makes it into a negative sign manifesting the old scar of exaggerated division between clergy and lay.

"I'm still not going to drink from the cup! AIDS, hepatitis, you know, and the other things you can catch . . ." may remain our attitude despite the good symbolism. The spread of Acquired Immune Deficiency Syndrome is indeed a terrible danger and cause for considerable fear. Arguments about the cup being a better symbol of unity may seem of little weight in comparison. Nor is the notion that God would not let anyone get AIDS from the communion cup one that helps many of us. At the moment the atmosphere is so charged with apprehension that we are probably not able to consider anything but the awful threat of AIDS.

Yet there are a few things to consider. Contrary to the long-held notion, medical science has discovered that the concentration of germs in our mouths is lower than it is on our hands. There is less risk of spreading communicable diseases by mouth than by day to day hand contact. With regard to the spread of the AIDS virus, official warnings have not included the avoidance of shared eating utensils, drinking cups and the like. In fact, some would argue that persons susceptible to infections, like AIDS victims, are safer receiving communion from the cup than receiving a host touched by another person's hands or laid in one's own hands.

But of a more serious nature, our refusing to receive communion from the cup may be motivated by the dread we have of the AIDS victims themselves. Many opinions around us intensify this dread by insisting on the complete isolation of infected persons. Because of the homosexuality and drug abuse associated with the disease, there are even undertones of the isolation being a deserved punishment. Court orders abound trying to protect victims from irrational demands for their separation from society, demands far beyond anything required by any real threat of infectiousness.

Our Christian identity may not require us to imitate the missionary, Father Joseph Damien, and take the risks he took living among the lepers of Molokai. On the other hand, we cannot give ourselves over to exaggerated fears either, and allow ourselves to be blind to everything but our own well-being and self-preservation.

Very basic to Christian values is the admonition that we would never join in the judgment of others no matter how guilty they may seem. Instead we are called to behave with understanding and compassion, especially toward the undesirables, those rejected and harshly treated. We cannot turn our backs on any human being. It is part of God's call to communion and unity.

Here is the more weighty question for us. Our decision about communion from the cup may mask an attitude that touches very seriously the Christian person we are called to be. It may make it impossible for our eucharistic celebration to join us into the one body of Christ. Efforts to have safe health methods in our sacramental practices are very important. But we must be very careful that our seeming concerns for safety do not hide attitudes that make it very difficult for us to be drawn into the unity God wills.

Other Helps

Besides giving a new emphasis to the central symbol, the general instruction also restores the procession and song to the communion rite in order to highlight its unifying force. The unity of voices which comes about in song is to give outward expression to "the communicants' union in spirit" (GI 56i). The song is also to make the procession "more fully an act of community" (GI 56i). Careful selection and implementation of the song can make it an expression of the unity occurring in the communion moment. But lining up for communion usually remains a queue rather than becoming a procession. Very few communicants experience the communion line as anything beyond its functional purpose. Using familiar music or hymns with easily learned antiphons so that people need not carry hymnals on their way to communion does encourage the singing. And stronger singing helps to create a feeling of common purpose to the movement. An adequate number of communion ministers also helps because it eliminates excessive delays in the line. But more pastoral ideas are needed. The key has not yet been found.

The general instruction also provides a silent time of prayer following the procession. The time should be explained so that it will be appreciated as a shared silence. It can be a rich moment of communion with the Lord, with our sisters and brothers in the faith and with all of humanity. But because it is a most intimate moment for us, the moment has often been left as a time of exclusive private communion with the Lord alone. Kneeling and covering our eyes with our hands, the posture once recommended, was strong body language that encouraged the attitude of exclusive communion. The posture recommended now of sitting in silence with an awareness of the people around us is not intended to tear anyone away from the Lord's presence. Rather it literally opens our eyes to the full communion to which the Lord calls us.

EUCHARISTIC MINISTERS

Ministers of the eucharist have a particular responsibility to help establish communion among the members of the assembly. It is their charge to make the communion moment into a greater moment of human communion, thus providing a better sacramental sign of communion with the Lord.

Jesus as we see him in the New Testament readily became involved with people. He was friend and teacher to his disciples, loving them and being loved by them in return as we love our friends. He was not a distant, vague figure to them as he sometimes seems to us. People were always important to Jesus. He never passed by any of them. The children were welcome in his company although the disciples would have preferred to chase them away. Lame beggars who called out to Jesus over the objections of the disciples received his attention. The grieving, those in whatever need, always found compassion, understanding and love from Jesus.

Communion with the Lord is with this Jesus who so readily engaged himself with people. The sacrament is the invitation to personal communion with him. Sometimes this fact is obscured by the abstract concepts we use to describe it, like sanctifying grace, eternal life or salvation. We forget that they are all ways of describing personal communion with the Lord. The eucharistic minister enfleshes that invitation of the sacrament. Through our personal presence to each other in the moment of communion we are sacraments which make present the welcoming Lord.

Although we are sometimes called dispensers of the eucharist, vending machine ways are out of order. The sacramental sign depends upon the minister treating the communicant with simple human dignity. It means no more than catching the person's eye, speaking to the person and listening to the person's response, then gently offering the host or cup. Having the host slapped into one's hand or driven into one's mouth gives the impression that the other occupation of the minister is in the forest cutting timber. Timber cutters are usually paid by the piece. The greater number of logs cut brings a bigger paycheck at the end of the week. Some eucharistic ministers will be surprised to discover that having dispensed 312 hosts will not merit a greater reward than if they had dispensed a mere 125.

Eucharistic ministers must be personal and person-centered as Jesus is. They need to like people and have a welcoming attitude toward them, able to care for them. The minister must also be at ease with people, able to look them in the eye with comfort and to touch them without embarrassment. We recognize in these qualities of a good eucharistic minister the person who can bring people, even strangers, together. The care and respect this person gives to other people makes them feel part of the gathering.

In plain human terms such a eucharistic minister does much to unify an assembly. But in the total reality of the moment, we know that the simple human communion established is in fact a sacramental sign of communion with the Lord, the source of all communion in the assembly.

CONCLUSION

The hunger for human communion is very deep within all of us. We all need to feel that we belong to someone. Many things in modern day society threaten our sense of belonging. Our big cities can seem so vast and impersonal. In them we can easily feel on the edge of loneliness and despair. No wonder there was an enthusiasm when "experiencing community" became a possibility for the liturgy. Unfortunately the enthusiasm led us into some adolescent pitfalls, and now there is a reaction against the "craze for community."

The better answer is to follow the *General Instruction of the Roman Missal.* It provides for an experience of community, the unified assembly. But it is always insistent that the faith bonds are foremost. Whatever human communion we may experience in the liturgy, it is always to be an expression of the deeper communion of faith to which we are called. But our communion of faith needs to be experienced and expressed in human terms. Only then is the assembly an effective reality in the world.

Our experience of human communion, through the guidelines of the general instruction, becomes an experience of the unified assembly. The assembly is the church gathered by God, the only lasting, ultimately meaningful community.

3.

The Entire Assembly Celebrating:
Engaging Lay Persons

Engaging lay persons is a special question which comes up when we talk about forming the unified assembly as we celebrate the eucharist. Most of us who gather together into the assembly are among the laity. Today a typical parish has many of its lay persons involved in the celebration. The lay, liturgical ministries have been expanded to include lectors and special ministers of the eucharist. In many parishes lay persons also take part in the planning of the celebration, are responsible for scheduling the liturgical ministers and share in other preparation details. Likewise as members of the congregation lay persons are expected to take a very active part in the celebration. *The General Instruction of the Roman Missal* encourages all of this active involvement.

But for years lay people were expected to sit quietly and meditate if they were not a server, usher or choir member. So the questions arise: Is all this activity proper? Should the general instruction have encouraged it? Is it being allowed as a stopgap until the clergy can regroup? There also are some members of the congregation who prefer things as they were. Sitting passively in the pew, they resist the attempts made to engage them.

Being part of a unified assembly would seem to require all of us to be fairly active. It would be a little strange if we were all called together, but the larger part of us were made to appear as though we were mere spectators.

The work of this chapter will be to see what foundations there are for the active role which the general instruction now assigns to those among us who are the laity. We will need to look first at some liturgical principles from the *Constitution on the Sacred Liturgy*. The constitution had been very definite. Lay people were not to be present for the eucharist "as strangers or silent spectators" (CSL 48). But discussion of principles will be only the first step. As in the last chapter we will follow the lead of the general instruction and spend most of our time looking at parts of the actual celebration. They will be the parts to which the general instruction gives a special lay bias.

From these discussions we will come to understand how the general instruction expects lay persons to be incorporated into the celebration. Only then with all members actively engaged does a truly unified assembly result.

ACTIVE PARTICIPATION FOR EVERYONE

Active participation is the first principle we need to consider from the constitution:

> Mother Church earnestly desires that all the faithful be led to that full, conscious, and active participation in liturgical celebrations which is demanded by the very nature of the liturgy (CSL 14).

For our concern, the words "all the faithful" are the important ones. We inherited a liturgy in which priests did almost everything. There was never any doubt about their active participation. Thus the real impact of this principle of the Second Vatican Council was on lay people. As the council understood the nature of the liturgy, everyone who assembled for the celebration, both clergy and lay, was to have active parts.

This is quite a contrast from the way the role of lay people used to be explained. While the priest said all of the prayers, read the scriptures and carried out all the rites, we were instructed to meditate on what he was doing. The sacramentary provided no parts for us and made only passing references to us. It was almost entirely concerned with the actions of the priest.

Meditating on the mass is certainly a fruitful form of participation, but it does leave us outside of things a little bit. It has us watching what someone else is doing. There is something to be said for having a part in actually doing some of the ritual. It is like an audience watching a play or hearing a concert. They are engaged and participating but not like the actors and musicians. Nor does the power of the play or music touch the audience as it does the performers.

Active participation aims at getting all of us engaged like those performers. Vatican II judged that it was no longer an adequate participation for lay people to watch devoutly while the priest performed the rites. Lay people are to be actively involved in a similar way like the priest.

Active Participation—Our Right

In order to give this kind of participation to lay people, the council had to overcome one serious obstacle. For a long time it was thought that only ordained persons could be so active in carrying out the liturgy. On what basis could Vatican II now claim a similar right for lay people?

The council continued to see the sacrament of orders as empowering a person for a particular role within the celebration. But it also restored the understanding of baptism as fundamental in establishing the right—and obligation—for active participation in the liturgy. "Such participation . . . is their right and duty by reason of their baptism" (CSL 14). This is true for clergy as well as laity. For all of us, baptism, not ordination, is the foundation of our right to be active in the liturgy.

Baptism is this foundation for two reasons: it brings entry into the church, and it gives us a share in the priesthood of Christ. These reasons are stated in another of the documents from the Second Vatican Council, the *Dogmatic Constitution on the Church:*

> Incorporated into the church through baptism, the faithful are consecrated by the baptismal character to the exercise of the cult of the Christian religion (DCC 11).

> For their part, the faithful join in the offering of the eucharist by virtue of their royal priesthood (DCC 10).

Baptism, Our Share in Priesthood

Most of us knew we became members of the church when we were baptized. But it is a surprise to hear that our baptism also gives us a share in Christ's priesthood. In our common notions, only an ordained person was considered a priest. It was not realized that baptism gives all of us a priestly nature. It is not the same as an ordained person, but still a true priesthood.

If we go back to the paragraph of the *Constitution on the Sacred Liturgy,* which gave us the principle of active participation, we find that it quotes 1 Peter 2:9: ". . . you are a chosen race, a royal priesthood, a holy nation . . ." (#14). Scripture experts now generally agree that 1 Peter had its origins in homilies preached on the occasion of baptism. Thus, "a royal priesthood" would not refer to the ordained but to the baptized. Later in the same constitution, another paragraph talks about how individual members are involved differently in the liturgical celebration (CSL 26). It makes a lot of distinctions, but it does not distinguish between priest and non-priest. According to Vatican II, we all share in the priesthood of Christ through our baptism. As a priestly people we actively participate in the liturgy.

Made members of the church through baptism and given a share in Christ's priesthood, we can all take an active part in the celebration of the eucharist. Now we can fully realize the priority of gathering together.

LAITY INCLUDED IN THE HIERARCHICAL NATURE OF THE LITURGY

The hierarchical nature of the liturgy is the other principle we need to examine from the *Constitution on the Sacred Liturgy.* We probably have some familiarity with this principle and do not realize it. Articles about the church in Catholic newspapers and magazines often will make some mention of the "hierarchy." These actually are references to the hierarchical ordering of the church. From that ordering of the church, the liturgy gets its hierarchical nature. But the references are often very limited in meaning and indicate only the special authority and leadership which the pope, bishops and priests have in the church.

The principle actually refers to much more. It states how the whole church is organized around the bishops. Basically, as members of the church all of us carry out our different responsibilities and tasks under his direction, or, more immediately, under the direction of our pastors who represent the bishop to us. We do not simply follow our own private inspirations.

Fulfilling our ministries under the direction of the bishop is what hierarchical ordering means. It assures unity within the church, that quality so essential to what the church is. As hard as it may be, all the ministries and service we do must be brought together into the one work of the church. They cannot be separate, individual missions of evangelization, charity and the like. The church hierarchically organized helps to bring about that unity.

The constitution applies this principle to the liturgy. Just as in all the work of the church, so in the liturgy our many ministries must be brought together into one, unified celebration:

> Liturgical services are not private functions, but are celebrations of the church, which is the "sacrament of unity," namely, a holy people united and organized under their bishops (CSL 26).

The general instruction spells it out in more definite terms. A communal celebration of the church requires various ministries. But these are arranged in a hierarchical structure. Thus, even though diverse, they "at the same time form a complete and organic unity" (GI 257).

Like active participation, the real impact of the constitution stating a principle of hierarchical ordering was on lay people. The clergy were secure in the hierarchy of the church. This is evident from the way the word "hierarchy" is so often used. But properly, as the organizing principle of the church body, hierarchy includes the laity. This is a surprise to many.

Restoring the hierarchically ordered place of lay people in the liturgy is a very prominent concern for the constitution when it takes up the reform of the liturgy. In its section about the reform entitled, "Norms Drawn from the Hierarchic and Communal Nature of the Liturgy," lay people are mentioned several times.

The preferred celebration of the eucharist and of all the sacraments is one that has lay people present and participating (CSL 27). The lay ministries exercised within the celebrations are "a genuine liturgical ministry" (CSL 29). The constitution also mentions that the acclamations, responses, psalms, antiphons and hymns are to be done by the people (CSL 30).

We take it for granted. But some of us would remember when things like the Lord, have mercy, Glory to God and the Holy, holy were recited by the priest while the choir or congregation sang them. The duplication of these parts by the priest was considered their official recitation, necessary for the integrity of the rite. More than we realize, the new assignment of these parts is a recognition that lay people have a place in the hierarchical ordering of the liturgy.

Finally, the sacramentary is to include rubrics (directions) outlining the people's part in the celebration (CSL 31). Already we have mentioned how sacramentaries once contained only directions for the priest's part. Including rubrics for the people is another establishing of their legitimate, hierarchical place in the liturgy.

Restoring the hierarchical place of lay people in the liturgy actually recognizes their holiness. For us, as we have seen, "hierarchy" signifies authority, ordering and unity. But if we were to go back to the origins of the word, we would find that it is derived from the Greek word for "holy." Close to this original meaning is the English word "hierarch," denoting a person who has authority in sacred things. Thus to recognize the place of lay people in the hierarchy is also to recognize their holiness and their legitimate authority to participate in the liturgy.

Subsidiarity—Respecting Each Other's Role

Besides bringing together the many ministries of the liturgy into a unified celebration, the hierarchical nature also includes a respect for the diversity of roles. This aspect of the principle is known as subsidiarity. By subsidiarity, though, something else is meant besides the usual definition of secondary or subordinate. Here it simply means that we are not to infringe on the parts belonging to other members of the assembly as we carry out our own part in the celebration (CSL 28). The caution goes back a long way in the tradition of the church. Pope Clement of Rome, in the year 100, spoke about the hierarchical ordering of the eucharist. All were to have their role including lay people, and no one was to transgress that appointed role (*Letter to the Corinthians*).

Subsidiarity applies to everyone active in the liturgy. It would be a safeguard if the active participation of the laity were ever to take on an exaggerated importance. But the real force of subsidiarity, like the hierarchical principle itself, was to help find a place for lay people in the celebration. The clergy accustomed to doing all the important parts themselves were the ones for whom the caution brought the greatest adjustment. Subsidiarity finds expression in the general instruction with a specific directive concerning lectors. They have their own proper function, and should exercise it even when an ordained person may be available to read (GI 66). The function should never be taken over by the ordained person, as sometimes happens when more than one priest is present for the celebration (GI 66). Nor should the presence of a seminarian make any difference. Lay lectors are still the proper persons to proclaim the first two readings.

LAY PARTICIPATION ASSURED

We can easily find principles of active participation and the hierarchical ordering of the liturgy in the general instruction. They clearly are organizing principles for it. Built upon these principles the *General Instruction of the Roman Missal* is very forceful in assuring an active place for lay people. In its opening paragraphs the instruction is very emphatic about the celebration being carried out by the entire assembly, an assembly hierarchically organized with a particular place for the laity. The first paragraph begins by identifying the celebration as "the action of Christ and the people of God arrayed hierarchically" (GI 1). The next one makes it specific that "the people of God" means the ministers and the faithful together taking their proper parts (GI 2). In the third paragraph, the planning of the celebration is to have special regard for the participation of the faithful (GI 3). Jumping ahead to Chap-

ter III of the instruction which takes up the "Offices and Ministries" necessary for the celebration, we find one described for the
faithful (GI 62–64).

Throughout the instruction references continue to be made
about the part lay people should have in the celebration. The
instruction rarely uses the term "laity" though. It prefers "the
faithful" (GI 62) or simply "the people" (GI 99).

Alert to this vocabulary, we can find mention of the laity in
almost every paragraph describing a part of the mass. Paragraphs
either describe a part properly done by the people (GI 26, 28, etc.)
or the significance of the part for them (GI 24, 25, etc.). The
paragraphs concerning architecture include the requirement of a
place reserved for the faithful, and go to some detail in describing
how this location should encourage the participation of the people
(GI 257, 273).

The sacramentary itself now contains the acclamations and
responses for the people's part. Remembering how once sacramentaries only contained texts to be recited by the priest, we
can appreciate what an innovation this is. The laity now very defi-
nitely have a recognized, active part in the celebration of the
eucharist.

Establishing this active role required both principles, active
participation and the hierarchical ordering of the liturgy. These
need to go hand in hand. Indeed, we find that the general instruction usually mentions them together. Whenever it speaks of the
celebration being the activity of all the members, it generally mentions that the roles are hierarchically ordered (GI 1, 2, 58, 257,
297). Without a re-emphasis on the hierarchical ordering, active
participation re-establishing an active role for the laity could seem
to be introducing conflict. It could seem to jeopardize the essential
participation of the ordained priest. But alert to the hierarchical
ordering of the liturgy, we see how the role of lay persons fits into
the whole liturgy and does not undermine the unity of the
celebration:

> All in the assembly gathered for mass have an individual
> right and duty to contribute their participation in ways
> differing according to the diversity of their order and

liturgical function. Thus . . . the very arrangement of the celebration itself makes the church stand out as being formed in a structure of different orders and ministries (GI 58; cf. GI 257).

We are ready now to talk about specific parts of the mass and how lay participation should be highlighted in the way we do them. The general instruction describes two parts as especially lay oriented. They are the general intercessions and the preparation of the gifts.

GENERAL INTERCESSIONS

The lay slant to the general intercessions is reflected in its alternate name, "prayer of the faithful," the name we more commonly use (GI 45). The general instruction actually identifies the prayer of the faithful as a time when the laity exercise their priestly function and "intercede for all humanity" (GI 45).

The kinds of petitions to be included also show us how this part is to have a special association with lay members of the assembly. There are always to be included petitions for public officials and for people in any kind of need (GI 45, 46). These petitions, for the well-being of human life here on earth, bring up the political and economic side of things. A Christian influence in these realms has traditionally been considered the mission particular to lay people in the church. The petitions become an occasion for us to bring our lay mission explicitly into the prayer of the eucharist.

During special parish celebrations this could be done in a solemn way. Representatives of parish groups which address political questions or who work with people in need, like Christian service or peace and justice commissions, the Vincent DePaul Society, the Legion of Mary or Right to Life groups, could come forward at the proper time to voice individual petitions for their special work.

In all celebrations the petitions should be made by someone from the congregation (GI 47, 99). The presider encourages the assembly and prays the concluding oration, but making the petitions belongs to the people (GI 33).

A preference, though, is stated for a deacon to lead the petitions (GI 47). But this does not really detract from their lay orientation. Traditionally the deacon gave the congregation its cues and led its responses. Thus, a deacon leading the petitions still keeps them a congregational part. The preference could also reflect the prominence which the deacon should have in caring for the temporal needs of the poor. It is another dimension which relates the petitions especially to the faithful. They are the ones who provide the church with the means to care for temporal needs and charity. With many parishes being served by permanent deacons, we need to understand the preference properly. Otherwise it could appear to be an unnecessary clerical infringement.

By all means, whenever a congregation is present, there should be a prayer of the faithful. The general instruction is very strong about it (GI 45). It is a key moment when the active participation of the faithful is given expression. It should not be set aside.

PREPARATION OF THE GIFTS

We have already taken one look at the preparation of the gifts in the previous chapter. It was one of those three major changes made in the way we celebrate mass. The change shifted the preparation of the gifts away from being something done almost entirely by the priest. The preparation is now to include bringing up the gifts by representatives of the congregation. The change made the preparation of the gifts an activity involving the whole gathering, an action that builds the unified assembly.

We also need to consider the preparation of the gifts from the standpoint of incorporating lay participation. The importance for representatives of the congregation to carry out their part must be underlined. Twice the general instruction mentions the appropriateness of the faithful presenting the bread and wine (GI 49, 101). Any part designed to engage lay people deserves special attention. But this part is one of the few times when lay people have actions to do in the celebration. Usually their participation is limited to speaking the words of the acclamations and responses, and to taking the postures of the congregation, standing, sitting, kneeling, etc. With actions so seldom assigned to lay people, we must be careful with the ones that are given to them.

It is very important to have someone responsible for asking members of the congregation to bring up the gifts. The invitation should be given beforehand. Many people see it as a privilege and they want time to prepare internally, and externally. The person responsible should telephone a few days in advance of the celebration. If a particular family has someone deceased or some other special intention to be remembered at the mass, then members of that family are the ideal persons to invite.

The general instruction also mentions the ancient practice of the faithful bringing the bread and wine from their homes for the liturgy (#49). It further notes that while this is no longer the practice, still the rite "retains the same spiritual value and meaning."

The meaning spoken of here is somewhat like bringing cookies to the bake sale. Contributing something of our own increases our personal investment in the project. The bake sale is no longer a generic event of the parish but one in which we find ourselves interested and involved. It is now a project which belongs to us.

In order for the preparation of the gifts to retain a meaning like this, the bread and wine ought to have a closer identity with the lay members of the assembly. The bread and wine should be more like household items rather than sacred products of the convent or monastery. The gifts would then help to draw us into the action and would help to underline the preparation of the gifts as especially a lay part.

Once more it makes sense for a parish to have some of its members bake the eucharistic bread. Others could manage the wine supply, purchasing it from the supermarket rather than from a supplier of official church goods. There are regulations about the quality of wine used for the eucharist, but many table wines available on local store shelves meet the standards.

These suggestions are minor, hardly earth-shaking. But they would give a stronger sense of identity with the bread and wine to the laity, thus increasing lay ownership of the preparation of the gifts.

The general instruction also provides for money and other gifts to be collected and brought up by the faithful (GI 49, 101). Sometimes there is an embarrassment about doing such things. We feel that money is tainted and does not belong in the liturgy. Presenting foodstuffs or clothing for the poor is dismissed as excessively relevant. We need to give second thoughts to these attitudes. They disparage daily work, the source of money and the source of things for the poor. They imply the old notion that the day to day endeavors of life are too mundane to have a place in the eucharistic celebration.

Since the lives of lay people are usually very much occupied with daily work, the emphasis which the general instruction intends for the preparation of the gifts is at stake. Actually the whole place of lay people in the liturgy is called into question by these negative attitudes about other gifts being presented besides the bread and wine.

Not too long ago the monastic life or life in the convent, separated from worldly affairs, was presented to us as the only true, ideal way to live Christianity. The life of lay people with its secular cares was considered a compromise. As a result lay people present at mass were not considered worthy to have an active part in the sanctuary. We find a different attitude today. The Second Vatican Council affirmed a very wholesome understanding of daily work. According to the *Dogmatic Constitution on the Church* any honest daily labor can be offered to God as a pleasing sacrifice (DCC 34).

It had been our early tradition at the preparation of the gifts to present along with the bread and wine things for the poor. The teaching of Vatican II provided the necessary understanding so that the general instruction could recover the tradition. The teaching also removed any notions of lay people being unworthy to participate in the mass. We are closer to the spirit of the council and the general instruction if we follow the sentiments found in the prayers recited by the presider upon receiving the gifts. These prayers show a great respect for all the gifts of creation and for "the work of human hands," which helps shape those gifts.

We should note that we are speaking of money and gifts which can be actually used by the church and the poor. We are not speaking of purely symbolic gifts. The general instruction does not provide for that type of gift to be part of the presentation. Such gifts are best avoided, for they so often fall victim to the popular trends. They can also quickly turn the procession into a small parade. But of greatest significance, these items entirely of a symbolic nature detract from the truly great symbols of the bread and wine. Things for the church and the poor have their symbolic side, but are at last actual gifts of a tangible nature. Hence, they do not interfere or compete with the symbolism of the bread and wine the way purely symbolic gifts do.

There is another contrast to be drawn between purely symbolic gifts and gifts which can actually be used for the church or for the poor. Symbolic gifts, so often, center on a person. At funerals they usually represent aspects of the loved one's work, things the person cherished or something of what the person meant to us. The other popular use of symbolic gifts is to represent some aspect of ourselves, something of our inner dispositions or some Christian responsibility we have fulfilled and now are bringing to the celebration.

By contrast gifts for the church or for the poor, especially, represent love and care for others. They do not center on ourselves or someone dear to us as the symbolic gifts tend to do. Anything which helps us to show concern for others rather than ourselves is the better choice for the Christian. It is also the choice necessary if the gathering of the whole Christian community is to be realized.

THE EUCHARISTIC PRAYER

Lay members of the assembly now are to participate even in the eucharistic prayer, "the center and summit of the entire celebration" (GI 54). Because the prayer is so central to the celebration, reciting it has always been reserved in a special way to the presider. For us this has always meant the ordained priest. The general instruction continues to assign it to him (GI 10). But, in carrying it out, the priest now "invites the people" and "unites them with himself in the prayer" (GI 54). "The meaning of the prayer," according to the instruction, "is that the *entire congregation* joins itself to Christ" (GI 54).

In the eucharistic prayer itself, the memorial acclamation and the great Amen have been added. The prayer already had opened with a dialogue. Now interspersed with these additional responses, the eucharistic prayer clearly is one to be led by the presider, but in association with the assembly.

Incorporating lay people to the eucharistic prayer has a very great significance for lay participation. In fact it helps to advance a new understanding of the lay state.

Lay persons no longer are considered compromised members of the assembly because they live in the world and are engaged in its day to day affairs. But living in the world continues to be used as an identifying characteristic of the laity. It is the traditional identity and underscores how the priesthood of the faithful should be exercised primarily in the sanctifying of daily life. The first responsibility of lay people is to be a Christian presence in the world.

Involvement in things like the liturgy must never occupy the laity to such an extent that their "worldly" vocation is neglected. The emphasis is important and needs to be recalled especially today because the current enthusiasm for liturgical ministries could distort what should be the first concern.

With regard to the liturgy, though, the traditional identity of lay people usually has carried with it a limitation that is not so appropriate. It is used to suggest that they exercise their priesthood solely in the sanctifying of daily life. Although they have some participation in the liturgy, the truly holy parts are to be done by the ordained priest.

Today a new perspective moderates this limiting notion. The new perspective actually arises from a challenge to the traditional lay identity itself. For one thing the lifestyles of clergy and also religious have taken on more secular features. They too live "in the world" and have duties there. Lay people for their part have been given many more direct responsibilities for "church work." They could always volunteer to help in CCD programs or in charitable projects, but now we find many of the laity organizing and directing these things. The great number of lay persons who are directors of religious education would be a case in point. That kind of responsibility was generally thought to belong to the clergy and religious. It was an exception for a lay person to be found with it. The lines are blurred, and it no longer seems appropriate to assign the duty of sanctifying daily life to lay persons alone, nor to leave church affairs solely to clergy and religious.

From another perspective we are appreciating how the church itself exists "in the world" and has a mission to the world. The church apart from the world, rescuing people from the temptations of temporal life, is an image of the church which has its value. But it is an incomplete notion. The mission of the church to the world must be part of the picture. As a result, no member of the church can ignore the world or escape from it. The whole church is to sanctify daily life. All of us share in this mission, not just the lay members.

There are of course divisions of labor in the church. The distinctions of clergy, religious and lay still apply. But we can no longer consider one of them the secular branch of the church who alone takes care of the world while the others take care of the spiritual life.

Vatican II reaffirmed the traditional identity of lay people (DCC 31, 34). Consequently the association of laity with daily work figures large in the general instruction. We have seen it in our discussions about the prayer of the faithful and the preparation of the gifts.

But by giving lay persons a participation in the eucharistic prayer, the general instruction also captures the new understanding of the lay state. The instruction is explicit. Having a place in the eucharistic prayer means lay people share in the actual offering of the eucharistic sacrifice (GI 54, 55f). They are to "offer the victim not only through the hands of the priest but also together with him" (GI 62). The presider, for his part, "joins the people to himself in offering the sacrifice" (GI 60).

The prayer of the faithful and the preparation of the gifts are parts belonging especially to the people. The general instruction, though, does not limit lay participation to these preliminaries. It also assigns a part in the real work of the liturgy, the eucharistic prayer. Now it is clear that active participation of the faithful does not come to an end once the preparations are completed, but continues into the heart of the eucharist. Lay persons are not limited to an exercise of their priesthood only in offering the sacrifice of daily life, but complete that offering by exercising their priesthood in the eucharistic sacrifice as well.

Further along, the general instruction encourages that all who receive communion would receive from hosts consecrated at the same mass and that we would also receive from the chalice when it is permitted. In this way communion would clearly be "a sharing in the sacrifice actually being celebrated" (GI 56h). We have discussed both practices before. Here is another reason for recommending them. They give expression to the full priesthood of the laity.

Returning to the eucharistic prayer, the lay part is carried out by listening reverently and by making the acclamations (GI 12, 55). We have already seen from other perspectives how both silence and the acclamations have an importance and deserve special care. As the way of lay participation in the eucharistic prayer, they become especially significant. There is plenty of reason for planning them carefully and doing them well.

Increasing the number of acclamations is often advanced as a way to make the eucharistic prayer more effective. What acclamations represent for lay participation recommends the suggestion. We realize that the acclamations are much more than a method to keep people alert during a long recitation. While we are not free to add acclamations, the eucharistic prayers intended for children's liturgies (contained in the most recent edition of the sacramentary) may be used in any celebration. These have many more acclamations than do the four regular eucharistic prayers. From time to time using these children's prayers would give us some experience with multiple responses. It would help us with our judgment when the time comes and further developments are permitted.

Even though lay participation in the eucharistic prayer has great significance, still it does not wipe out the unique role of the ordained priest. Reverent silence punctuated with acclamations provides a balanced way of participation that respects the role of the ordained and the role of the faithful. The entire assembly reciting the second eucharistic prayer does not. It is an exaggeration that confuses things. It may appear to implement the principle of active participation, but it certainly does not respect the hierarchical nature of the liturgy. It is not offered as an option in the general instruction.

The instruction makes the priest responsible for inviting the people into the eucharistic prayer. But it implies a complementary duty for those of us who assemble as the congregation. We have the responsibility to accept the invitation. It is very difficult for the priest to pray the eucharistic prayer adequately if we are not encouraging him with our alert, faith-filled attention. Members obviously absorbed in the prayer make up for the few who stare nowhere in particular, their eyes unfocused and their faces slack without expression. We must realize how our way of accepting the invitation affects the presiding priest. It is our responsibility to strengthen him by the way we participate in the eucharistic prayer.

THE COMMUNION RITE

Another topic first brought up in the last chapter was the communion rite. There its great significance for unifying the assembly was our concern. It holds a central importance for the discussion of active, lay participation as well. Active participation, according to the *Constitution on the Sacred Liturgy,* reaches a certain perfection in the receiving of communion (CSL 55).

Regular communion was restored to lay people long before the constitution or the general instruction was written. Now most of the congregation usually receives communion. The general instruction continues to encourage everyone to receive the Lord's body and blood as long as they are properly disposed (GI 56).

As a form of active participation, a number of things have come about to help us appreciate an active role in receiving communion. Standing for communion and making the "Amen" response are two of the well-established ones. In contrast to kneeling which makes us somewhat immobile, a standing posture has us ready for movement. Kneeling can be appropriate, for it beautifully expresses a humble, receptive attitude toward the great gift of the eucharist. But the general instruction encourages us to stand for communion (GI 21). As an active posture, standing expresses the response God calls forth in us as we receive the Lord's body and blood.

We take the "Amen" response for granted because it has long been restored to the communion rite. But before it was returned to us, the priest would bless the communicant with a prayer while the communicant remained silent and received the host. Like standing, the "Amen" allows us a chance to express our active response to the gift of the eucharist.

Two features of more recent origin, communion in the hand and communion from the cup, also enhance our active part in the communion rite. The greater activity is quite evident in our hands upraised to accept the Lord's body or stretched out to receive the precious blood.

These two ways of receiving communion, besides being more active, also have a connotation that brings out the priestly quality of lay participation. For so long the ordained priest alone took the host into his hands and drank from the cup. Because these gestures were long associated with only him, they have gained the connotation of being priestly gestures. Thus when lay members of the assembly choose to receive communion in these ways, the gestures convey a priestly quality to their actions. The old restriction works to our advantage. Receiving communion in the hand and drinking from the cup when done by lay persons is an affirmation that they too share in the priesthood of Christ.

The elimination of the communion rail also encourages lay persons to be more active and identifies their participation as priestly. Without a communion rail the place of celebration does not give the appearance of being two separated areas, one in which the celebrant moves, another from which the congregation watches. It also eliminates any impressions of the assembly being divided into priestly and non-priestly members.

A recommendation from *Environment and Art in Catholic Worship* about decorating the church reflects the same concern. It recommends that we decorate the whole space rather than just the altar area (EACW 103). The decorations will then enhance the "unity of the celebration space and the active participation of the entire assembly" (EACW 103). We could also add that it will especially highlight the participation of the faithful as priestly.

Communion, the Real Purpose of the Eucharist

But the contribution of the general instruction to an active communion rite for the faithful lies beyond these individual items. It is found in the overall structure given to the liturgy of the eucharist. As the general instruction describes it, the whole action culminates in communion (GI 48, MCW 48, cf. EACW 25).

If most of us had been asked, we probably would have answered that the consecration is the climax moment. It was at that moment that a hush would settle over the congregation. In Rome when the pope celebrated mass at St. Peter's Basilica, silver trumpets were even blown. We had been taught that the most important thing happening during mass was Jesus becoming present in this special way. At the moment of consecration he was here. Thus it was the great moment of the celebration.

Our communion was something separate. Sometimes we did not even appreciate that it had any connections with the mass. It was not uncommon to receive communion beforehand even if we were able to remain for the mass itself. Or when time was limited and the crowd large, the celebrant would return to the altar and conclude the mass while other priests continued to distribute communion.

Confusing the consecration as the climax of the celebration pushed the actions of the ordained priest to the center, for we knew that the consecration required his powers of ordination. Then with communion seeming to be disconnected from the celebration, the rest of us appeared merely to receive the fruits of what the priest had accomplished.

Now the general instruction makes clear that communion is integral to the celebration, in fact the climax of it. The consecration occurs so that all of us may receive communion. Jesus becomes present through the consecration and the whole eucharistic prayer so that we may enter into communion with him. All is accomplished; the celebration has achieved its purpose when we are brought into that union with the Lord.

An active posture in receiving communion is quite proper for us as lay people. It does not detract from the essential work of the priest but fits together with it. We actively receive the body and blood of the Lord in response to his presence brought about during the priest's recitation of the eucharistic prayer.

There should be no hesitation to use the active elements provided for us in the communion rite. Active in the preparation of the gifts, having a part in the eucharistic prayer, our active engagement comes to its culmination in communion.

HELPS TO INTERIOR PARTICIPATION

Because participation for lay people had been almost entirely interior, engaging them more fully in the eucharistic celebration has meant an emphasis on external forms. Our discussions have been mostly about words, gestures and things that the general instruction now assigns as their part. In contrast to the wholly interior participation once prescribed for lay members of the assembly, these new concerns of the instruction could appear to be nothing more than a fuss for externals. They could even appear to be a distraction from interior communion which is the true goal of the eucharist.

But the *Constitution on the Sacred Liturgy* and the *General Instruction of the Roman Missal* remind us that we enter the interior realm of the spirit through things we perceive with our senses (CSL 7, 59; GI 5). Ceremonies and rites are a means to interior participation, not a distraction from it. As Vatican II observed, the external signs of the liturgy nourish our faith and dispose us to receive grace (CSL 59). They cannot be dismissed as trivial details but deserve careful consideration.

Reflecting this realization about externals, the constitution always described the principle of active participation as "both internal and external," minds attuned to voices (CSL 19, 11). "Proper dispositions" are always involved (CSL 11). The constitution was insistent. Whenever it mentioned our active part in the liturgy, it always spoke of the need for us to be fully aware and conscious of what we were doing (CSL 11, 14, 48). To this end the constitution reminded our pastors of their responsibility to provide us with the necessary instruction (CSL 19).

Ultimately, as Vatican II saw it, the renewed, active role of lay people in the liturgy was a cooperation "with heavenly grace" (CSL 11). It was to bring a deeper, personal involvement in the mystery of salvation. It was hardly a concern for externals alone.

The general instruction for its part offers us considerable help so that celebrating the eucharist will deepen our faith lives. First it provides for intelligent participation by giving extensive explanations of the mass. Its directives not only guide the celebration but also describe the significance of the various parts showing connections between the regulations and the understanding. In this way the instruction makes it possible for us to grasp the spirit and meaning of the rite. Almost any paragraph from chapter II which describes the individual mass parts could serve as an example, but numbers 33 and 48 are especially good. They give an extensive introduction to the liturgy of the word and the liturgy of the eucharist.

But the instruction goes beyond an intellectual grasp of the ceremonies. In many instances it indicates the interior dispositions which should accompany the ritual activity. For example, the reading of scripture is to be heard "with reverence" (GI 9). "Attention and devotion" are to characterize the ministry of the presider (GI 13). The instruction also alludes to the qualities of life which should characterize a person participating in the liturgy. The presider should serve "with dignity and humility" in order to communicate "a sense of the living presence of Christ" (GI 60). The faithful, in turn, are to conduct themselves with a sense of reverence for God and with charity toward the others sharing in the celebration (GI 62).

The general instruction cannot be accused of simply making a lot of changes in the external details of the rite. It provides much help in making the parts of the mass more intelligible for us. It deepens our sense of what it is we are doing, and gives many indications of the lifestyle that must underlie our entering into the celebration.

The instruction emphasizes that the celebration should bring

"about in the faithful a participation in body and spirit that is conscious, active, full, and motivated by faith, hope, and charity" (GI
3). For the general instruction, engaging lay people means much
more than giving them a few gestures to make and responses to
say. Finally these external things are meant to engage us better in
the deep, interior things of the Christian life. They are for our
"spiritual well-being" (GI 5).

AN IMAGE OF THE CHURCH

All the various parts we have discussed which are designed to
restore the active role of lay people in the eucharistic celebration
are important for that reason in itself. Still there is a greater
significance to them.

Because lay people make up the larger part of the eucharistic
assembly, they need to be actively engaged if the gathering is to
have the appearance of a unified body. Thus only if they have an
active part does the assembly manifest the church, for the church
is a unified people, the body of Christ. Here is the greater
significance, the liturgy showing forth to the world the true nature
of the church.

As Vatican II saw it, a people united in Christ is essential to
what the church is. Back in the first chapter, this vision of the
Second Vatican Council for the church was the reason gathering
together had a priority in the eucharistic celebration. Here it
shows why engaging lay people in the celebration is so important.

As a result, when the general instruction describes the role of
the laity in overall terms, unity is its main concern. In one of the
paragraphs which takes up the "Office and Function of the People
of God," the faithful are warned

> . . . to shun any appearance of individualism or division,
> keeping before their minds that they have the one Father
> in heaven and therefore are all brothers and sisters to
> each other (GI 62).

In all that lay persons do during the celebration, the paragraph
continues, "They should become one body." When they carry out

actions in a uniform manner and assume uniform postures, "There is a beautiful expression of their unity" (GI 62). By entering into the common actions and common prayers we manifest the assembly as a unified body, a visible expression of the church.

The instruction is emphatic and explicit. People taking an active part in the eucharistic assembly "bring out more plainly the ecclesial nature of the celebration" (GI 4). Their participation when the bishop presides makes for "the pre-eminent expression of the Church" (GI 74; cf. GI 257, CSL 41).

4.

Liturgical Ministries: Enabling the Assembly

The priority of gathering together must have its place in the shaping of lay, liturgical ministries. It has already changed the expectations placed upon the ushers. Concern that ushers would become greeters or hospitality ministers has its roots in the realization of how important gathering together is for the community. All liturgical ministers, though, need an appreciation of how their activities can serve the coming together of the assembly. They must see that a dimension of their ministry is to help the gathered community know its bonds of union.

This perspective is very useful in determining how liturgical ministries should be carried out. Moreover, it is very valuable in forming the attitudes of the liturgical ministers themselves. It can give them a sense of the community to which they belong and serve.

Liturgical ministers do not always have an adequate awareness of the community. Some think of their ministry as a way to fulfill their Christian duty, or as a response to a new-found zeal. The focus is on themselves. It is not obvious to them that their ministry serves the gathering.

At times lectors or eucharistic ministers are overly concerned about their personal worthiness. They do not realize that the needs of the assembly are the reason they have been given the ministry. Thus they trouble over their worthiness, without sufficient regard to how their service is needed in the gathering.

This chapter will consider each of the liturgical ministries and point out what they can contribute to the building of the unified assembly. In doing so the chapter should also help the liturgical ministers broaden their focus. It should become evident for them that in performing their ministries they are indeed serving the community.

"GENUINE LITURGICAL MINISTRY"

Before considering the individual ministries, more needs to be said about lay, liturgical ministers and their relationship to the assembly. Two aspects are involved. First, there is the realization that when a lay person carries out a particular role in the liturgy, it is a true ministry. Liturgical ministry was once the domain of the ordained priest. He was the one who "ministered" the sacraments to us. A lay person helping in the celebration, like an altar server, was considered a *minor* minister at best.

The second realization is that liturgical ministers serve the entire assembly. We used to think of lay persons as only helping the priest. Again altar servers, for example, were simply the priest's assistants. They were not seen to be in the service of the entire assembly.

The *Constitution on the Sacred Liturgy* corrected these notions. It recognized that lay persons who carried out particular tasks in the liturgy were true ministers:

> Servers, lectors, commentators, and members of the choir also exercise *a genuine liturgical ministry* (CSL 29).

The constitution likewise made clear that these ministries were to "God's people," not merely to the presider (CSL 29).

When the general instruction calls lay persons to particular roles in the celebration, it reflects the sentiments of the constitution. It designates these persons as "ministers" and indicates that their service is to the "people of God" assembled (GI 62).

There is dignity in being a minister to the Christian community. Respect for this dignity by the community and by liturgical ministers themselves can be a strength to the building of the unified assembly. The Christian community acknowledging the dignity of its lay, liturgical ministers gives them the support and strength they need to minister well in the gathering. If only the ordained priest is respected by the congregation and the lay ministers who serve the assembly are hardly noticed, it will be very difficult for these ministers to carry out their tasks with any kind of confidence and security. Insecure and unsure of their place in the gathering, lay persons can contribute little to the building up of the unified assembly.

To some extent this is the situation of communion ministers who experience individuals switching lines so as to receive communion from the priest. Persons are free to do so. Still the need to recognize the legitimate ministry which the lay minister exercises should cause second thoughts. Receiving communion from the lay person would indicate respect and acceptance of that ministry. It would help the whole congregation to appreciate how lay persons appropriately carry out ministries in the liturgical assembly.

For the liturgical ministers themselves, knowing their dignity should call forth competence and reliability. Servers or eucharistic ministers who frequently miss their assignments, or lectors who in their proclamations betray a two-minute preparation, are hardly persons who respect themselves as liturgical ministers.

Persons with that respect accept the responsibilities which are theirs. They realize that their service is necessary to the celebration and important to the assembly. They do not put their own interests and convenience before their ministries. However, if the Christian community does not respect all of its liturgical ministers, then it can only be grateful for whatever service they give. It cannot be critical about service done poorly or withheld entirely.

There is one more detail to be mentioned before moving on. Vesture and location in the assembly can help to signify that persons do not step out of their lay state when they fulfill a ministry in the liturgy. Robed lectors and eucharistic ministers may confuse the issue. It is better that they function in lay attire, i.e., looking like lay persons rather than junior clerics. Likewise seating lectors, eucharistic ministers and even altar servers in the congregation helps to keep their lay identity clear.

USHERS

Ushers deserve first concern as we begin considering how each of the liturgical ministries can contribute to the new priority of gathering together. What ushers have traditionally done at mass, as well as what they are now being encouraged to do—the rediscovered work of hospitality—can contribute so significantly to the building of the unified assembly.

Another reason they deserve to be first is the fact that for so long the ushers have been the "Cinderellas" of the liturgical renewal. While we were busy developing extensive training sessions for lectors and eucharistic ministers we neglected the ushers. They had to figure things out for themselves in this new liturgy. We may commission eucharistic ministers with a special ritual celebrated at one of the big masses on Sunday morning, but ushers are still commissioned with a tap on the shoulder: "Jerry didn't show up; will you take the left side?"

Now that we have rediscovered hospitality and would like the ushers to take a responsibility for it, we criticize them. We talk about them as the cronies who stand in the vestibule kibitzing among themselves while parishioners have to push their way through this crew of "greeters." Or we ask why the ushers must always scowl and make us feel as though we have just tried to sneak a smoke or lift someone's wallet? Impatient, we dismiss them as among the old guard, unwilling to change.

We forget in the rush of our criticism that many of the ushers are among the faithful, reliable parishioners upon whom the parish has often depended. Instead of criticism they deserve special care to help them understand the importance of the gathered assembly, and to show them how ushering can be effective in bringing it about.

Hospitality

Describing hospitality is a good starting point. It will allay fears and allow the ushers to consider what is being asked when they find themselves with the new names of "greeter" or "minister of hospitality."

In practical terms an usher's hospitality is simply a smile, a friendly greeting and maybe some small talk as parishioners arrive. It does not require any deep "I – thou" or articulate confession of faith. And it is certainly distant from any hugging or other tactile expressions that are now used by some who are more effusive about the bonds we ought to have as companions in the faith.

The more adept ushers may appropriately call persons by name, ask about family concerns and the like. Whatever an usher can do to show some personal care and human warmth to the persons entering the church doors is hospitality.

"Be hospitable to one another" is an admonition of the New Testament (1 Pet 4:9; cf. Rom 12:13). In the Old Testament the Jewish people are constantly urged to welcome the alien, the widow and the orphan (Ex 22:20–21; Lv 19:33; Dt 27:19). The chosen people were expected to be hospitable to these unfortunates. God's special kindness and favor to the chosen people was to spark in them a care and love for the victims of society. Hospitality was part of the covenant, no small matter.

Then there was the insistent graciousness of Abraham (Gen 18:1–8). Only later did he realize upon whom he had pressed his hospitality. A reference to it is found in the letter to the Hebrews: "Do not neglect hospitality, for through it some have unknowingly entertained angels" (Heb 13:2).

This advice from Hebrews has special significance for us in our efforts to build the unified assembly. Ultimately, Jesus present among us is the bond of union that brings us together. His presence is at the root of whatever hospitality we may show. To paraphrase Hebrews, our hospitality entertains Christ present in our gathered community. In John's gospel some Greeks approach Philip, asking him, "Sir, we would like to see Jesus" (12:21). The same request is being made of the ushers when they are asked to extend hospitality as the community gathers. "For where two or three are gathered together in my name, there am I in the midst of them" (Mt 18:20). Hospitable ushers are assisting that gathering in which Christ is present.

The church as a community is another perspective to help us understand what the ushers are doing when they offer hospitality.

Remember from our earlier discussion how the Second Vatican Council saw the church as essentially a communion of persons who were held together by their bonds of faith (Chapter 1). Further, this union of faith needed to be experienced and made manifest in the eucharistic assembly.

To this end, hospitality contributes two things, an atmosphere of belonging and an awareness of the other persons who gather with us. When these two things are occurring, we are able to experience the unity of our faith. From that experience we can draw motivation to behave toward each other in ways that will show forth the communion of the church.

Atmosphere of Belonging

"Parish family" was the idea we used to understand the teaching of Vatican II about the church as essentially a communion of persons. The parish family somewhat like a natural family should have some feelings for the ties that draw it together. This is what is meant by an atmosphere of belonging.

Being asked to promote this atmosphere, ushers are not being asked to propose something foreign. A sense of belonging to one's parish can already be found among parishioners. Even though persons readily change parishes these days, still most church-goers strongly identify one church or the other as their own. They speak of being from St. Anne's or St. John's parish, and have many reasons why they are attached and feel at home there. Some persons greatly dissatisfied with their parish begin considering a change, only to discover within themselves a loyalty that will not allow them to leave. Sometimes when a diocese must close a parish, the sense of belonging becomes very evident. Invariably feelings of great attachment are expressed by the members.

Ushers are actually helping parishioners to discover and deepen what is already present when they encourage an atmosphere of belonging. It is also something desired by the parishioners. City tourists will often report how delightful it was to attend mass in a small country parish. The friendliness of the people in the little church made it so easy to feel part of a parish family. Some of what these tourists find so attractive in the rural circumstances, ushers can help to create in a larger parish.

Enhancing an atmosphere of the parish family is not so difficult to do. When ushers engage parishioners in brief, casual conversation as they arrive, this atmosphere is being promoted. It does require the ushers to be present probably twenty minutes beforehand, but how important those twenty minutes can be to that sense of belonging! While having an outgoing personality can be helpful, it is not essential. They need only a healthy, positive attitude toward people and a willingness to exchange a simple "Good morning" with most of them.

As parishioners are leaving, the ushers again have a chance to build the atmosphere of belonging. Circumstances do not permit extended conversations, but there is time for a quick "Good-bye; see you next week." Such remarks are remembered and encourage people to return.

Husband–wife teams are especially effective for "door duty" because they give confidence to each other. We often see at parties how one spouse will encourage the other to talk with a particular individual. The security of having our spouse beside us may give us all the courage we need to be a greeter at the door.

The atmosphere of belonging must also incorporate the stranger, the person who is not a regular member of the parish community. There are bonds of faith with that person even though the human feelings of camaraderie are likely to be absent. Ushers can be the ones to extend the first hospitality. When a person is evidently an outsider, we ought to approach the person in an inviting way, introduce ourselves, then find the person a seat. If we are well acquainted with the assembly we should be able to spot some regular member in the congregation who is adept in making persons feel welcome and at home. It is ideal to seat the stranger next to one of these members. Of course, the usher should introduce the person and ask the member to help her/him be comfortable during the celebration.

Extending hospitality to visitors, though, must not be left to the ushers alone. Welcoming the stranger is a test of authenticity for all of us. Earlier we spoke of Abraham's being surprised when he realized to whom he had offered hospitality. According to the parable of the last judgment in Matthew's gospel, a similar surprise awaits those who welcome the outsider, an unpleasant surprise for those who do not (Mt 25:38, 43).

Coaxing the congregation to sit together is another task ushers can perform to help create that atmosphere of belonging. A congregation dispersed throughout the church as though we were the poor, lonely souls of purgatory will not give us the experience of being the Christian assembly. We will hardly feel united by our bonds of faith if we are seated alone in a pew distant from any other persons of the congregation. Only the gentle, good humored ushers should try this one. Being insistent in the wrong ways will bring more rancor than union.

Ushers, because they are very visible in the community, also help the parish family spirit by being examples of participation. Their very obvious entering into the common actions of the community, the singing, the prayers and responses, and the listening can greatly encourage others to do the same.

Finally it is sometimes necessary to remind ushers that they too belong. They are not exempt from the assembly. Ushers who roam and give the impression that what is going on does not concern them devastate the atmosphere of belonging.

Aware of One Another

Ushers can also spark an awareness of the persons who gather with us. This is the second aspect which hospitality contributes to our experience of the church in liturgy. When they speak to us as we enter, or when they introduce us to a visitor whom they may bring to sit with us, they are setting a tone of openness and approachability. We feel more like speaking to others, engaging them as we ordinarily would not. We are less fearful and have more courage to overcome our hesitation about persons not so well known to us.

Our awareness of the persons around us is also increased whenever ushers model personal care for another. Seeing an usher become attentive to someone who is ill, to an elderly person who needs help, or to the parent with a young child draws us to imitate that care. We are better disposed to notice others and to offer assistance with any immediate needs they may have.

We mentioned very early in our discussions how certain parts of the liturgy are now designed to summon us out of our individual prayer so that the presence of other persons is more evident to us (Chapter 1). Ushers, helping us to be aware of one another, provide the right frame of mind for these parts of the liturgy. We are better able to carry them out in a way that will achieve the purpose for which they were intended—to give us an experience of our unity in faith.

Joined together as we are, we cannot behave like tight-lipped strangers. This is true during the liturgy, especially when the church as a communion of persons should be experienced and made manifest. Assembled for eucharist we *must* pay attention to each other. The persons gathered with us need to have a place in our lives so that the church can be seen by the world.

It is a different situation if we are greeting passers-by on the street. It may be disheartening should they choose to be "hard of hearing" or refuse to look anywhere but straight ahead. Still they are completely within their rights if they prefer not to notice us. We have no claim over them. They do not belong to us in any special way.

Such is never the case with members of the Christian community. Our bonds of faith always require us to show some recognition and warmth for one another. The hospitable Jesus remains the example. His welcoming personality always allowed people to enter his life, be they children whom the disciples would have chased away, or public sinners who should not have been table companions.

Hospitality in all its aspects and the ushers who encourage it contribute greatly to what the liturgy is expected to be. *Environment and Art in Catholic Worship* declares with authority that "liturgy flourishes in a climate of hospitality" (#11).

The Usual Chores

In our enthusiasm for hospitality we must not overlook how the tasks usually done by the ushers also contribute to the building of the unified assembly. Three of these tasks deserve special note: tending to the comfort of the community, keeping order and taking up the collection.

The mundane comfort needs of the gathering may slip by as insignificant until the furnace is unattended and the building temperature falls to thirty-eight degrees. We may manage to get our hands from our pockets for the sign of peace, but little else will be done that day to celebrate our bonds of unity. The example shows us that the human need for some basic comforts affects how the magnificent theology of "where two or three gather in my name" will be accomplished.

Seeing that the lights are turned on, the ventilation or heat properly adjusted, and the correct hymnals and participation booklets passed out—the essential chores done by the ushers— are basic to any coming together of the community. These responsibilities are not minor details that can be pushed into the background by hospitality.

When St. Paul was visiting the Roman colony of Philippi, he was happy to hear Lydia of Thyatira say, "Come and stay at my house" (Acts 16:15). Now he had a place to preach and someone to care for the crowd. Ushers follow in the steps of Lydia, taking care of the comfort needs so that the crowd can become the gathered assembly. As Paul needed Lydia, the Christian community needs its ushers doing their usual, ordinary tasks.

In tending to the comforts of the community, ushers must also be alert to the whole celebration. If they are not, they can be detrimental to the work other ministers do in the building up of the assembly. For example the proclamation of the lector is destroyed if at the intense moment of the reading an usher marches down the center aisle beckoning two latecomers to follow.

There are other examples, but seating the late arrivals is the most frequent instance when ushers must be attentive to what else is happening in the liturgy. Alert to the entire celebration as it unfolds, ushers can find the slight breaks when movement is naturally going to occur, then seat the latecomers. After the opening prayer, the psalm response or after the alleluia verse would be the best times.

Ushers should also remember that the silent moments which follow the scripture readings are not breaks. They are the most inopportune times to bring in latecomers.

Keeping order was a need singled out by St. Paul: ". . . he is not the God of disorder but of peace" (1 Cor 14:33); ". . . everything must be done properly and in order" (1 Cor 14:40). We find ourselves more secure and ready to enter into the activity if we know what is going on. Confusion scares most of us. We become hesitant and unsure of ourselves, very reticent to become involved. The Christian community needs its officials in charge. When movement occurs during the gifts procession or at communion time, ushers directing the congregation insures the smooth running of things. It all contributes to a comfortable, secure atmosphere which encourages us to participate and to become the unified assembly. Earlier we had reason to emphasize the importance of the collection and the significance it has for lay participation. Its significance should redound to the ushers who gather it up. While representatives of the community ought to present the bread and wine, the ushers properly bring up the collection in the gifts procession. It is a moment when their service to the community can be recognized and appreciated.

MUSICIANS

Music has that bonding power which could be so forceful in building the unified assembly. Music is also that very effective form which active participation sometimes takes. But music's potential to gather us into one often goes unrealized in our liturgical celebrations. Here lies the task of the musician.

Faithful Servants Demoted

Long before gathering together was rediscovered, however, musicians were serving the Christian community. When few others were participating, musicians were adding beauty and solemnity to our worship. The ministry of music already deserves special respect and gratitude.

Unfortunately the first excitement about the assembly tended to demote these faithful servants of long standing. Even the enthusiasm for active participation, the very principle responsible for encouraging lay involvement, worked against them. It was the day of congregational singing. Accomplished musicians and choirs were only to support those melodies sung by all. For talented musicians, adding strength to the necessarily simple, congregational parts or even singing the descant was not enough to sustain their morale. Still we were emphatic that the general instruction identified the choir and other musicians as part of the congregation (GI 63, 274). Their task was to support the hymns, etc., sung by everyone.

It was a stunted interpretation to use the general instruction so narrowly. Besides encouraging the singing of the congregation, the instruction also sees the choir and other musicians having their "own liturgical function within the assembly" (GI 63). Indeed, they are part of the congregation, but with their own special role (GI 274). That role remains the uplifting of the entire assembly by providing a beauty and solemnity to the music (MCW 36). Without detracting from the importance of parts sung by all, the liturgy needs the inspiration of "great" music, music which demands a special competence (MCW 36).

All along the *Constitution on the Sacred Liturgy* had insisted, "Choirs must be diligently promoted" (114). The new priority does not diminish our need for expansive, joyful music that nourishes the human spirit. Music of that sort requires talented persons willing to practice.

New Facets to Music Ministry

On the other hand musicians must take into account the new priority too. They cannot continue to exercise their ministry as though all is as it were.

Three changes suggest themselves for the musically talented of the community. First, no mass should be without music. Persons responsible cannot plan the usual 11:30 choir mass, then have no one available with adequate musical abilities to sustain the singing of the other masses. Music is that important to the gathering of the assembly. The things done together, the acclamations and responses, best make us aware of our unity when we sing them. The entrance song and communion song have power to break us out of ourselves and to make us aware of our common bonds only if they are sung with strength and energy. Music can heighten the texts and make them "speak more fully and effectively. . . . It imparts a sense of unity to the congregation" (MCW 23).

Music unites us on a deeper level as well. It communicates the mystery of God present in the liturgy as few other things can (LMT 10). Our awareness of God present, calling us, is the reason we gather together in the first place. It is also the reason we are able to lay aside our divisions and become the unified assembly.

The priority of gathering together demands music. No longer can we think of music as merely adding beauty and solemnity, for then it is an option to the celebration. Knowing the importance of the unified assembly, the low mass or the recited mass without music is not a choice anymore.

The second change is that question of congregational singing. There is to be a place for it in every celebration (GI 63, 64; MCW 28, 36). Always there should be some music which the whole gathering is capable of singing together (MCW 28, 34). In selecting what parts to sing, a preference actually is to be given to elements that incorporate the congregation (GI 19). Never should all of the music be performed by the music minister, choir, folk group or soloist alone.

The rationale is not complicated. Anyone actively participating in the liturgy needs to sing (CSL 114; MCW 28). Listening is a partial and rather passive form of participation. Nor can a sense of the assembly be engendered by merely listening. We experience our unity when we give it full-throated expression. Those of us who are musicians know these things. We know how much more involved we are by singing or playing an instrument than by listening to someone else. We also know the bonds that develop among us from singing together in choirs and folk groups.

The third change requested of music ministers can be couched in words like those found in the first letter of John, "Share your joy" (1 Jn 1:4). We are told that music brings "joy and enthusiasm" to community worship (MCW 23). Indeed it must if it is going to have its unifying power over the assembly. But those of us who make up the greater part of the congregation do not experience music that way. For us the turnabout from listening to singing is hard work.

Music ministers, please help us to enjoy singing. Be patient with our negative attitudes. Keep coaxing and teaching us. Share with us your love for music so that we can come to appreciate the words of St. Augustine, "To sing belongs to lovers" (GI 19).

Choirs and Soloists

Providing the more intricate music which uplifts and swells the heart remains the special purpose of the choir and soloists. The importance of gathering together and becoming the unified assembly has not altered this traditional purpose, but it has brought a nuance.

The choir and soloists, we used to think, embellished the ceremonies, making them more solemn, more beautiful, by adding music. Now rather than embellish the ceremonies, the music of the choir and soloists is to serve the assembly. The purpose of excellent music is not simply to make the ceremonies more lovely, but to inspire and uplift the gathered community. We see the change in the music documents from our bishops which describe all music ministries as related to the congregation (MCW 35–38; LMT 64).

The nuance eliminates any notion of the elite performer and reinforces the ideal of dedicated service that should characterize church musicians (LMT 64). It also emphasizes that the choir and soloists need to carry out their roles in harmony with those of the other liturgical ministers. All are in the service of the one community.

Song Leaders and Cantors

Song leaders and cantors established to lead and sustain the singing of the congregation (GI 64) are especially important to the building of the unified assembly. They had not been a regular part of liturgical celebrations until the changes began to occur. Now the general instruction recognizes them and gives them definite ministries (GI 64).

In carrying out these ministries there is a danger that cantors and song leaders may interpret their roles as similar to that of the organist-soloist from the past. Those persons played and sang the parts of the liturgy which were to be sung. They simply provided the necessary music. Cantors and song leaders do not "provide music"; rather they encourage and help the whole community to express itself in song (MCW 35; LMT 68).

The effectiveness of a cantor or song leader was borne out in a recent study of parish worship. When a cantor or song leader is present, the study discovered, congregational singing becomes stronger.

Image of Unity

The priority of gathering together has given an overarching responsibility to all the musicians who serve the community. They are to be an image of unity for the whole assembly. This responsibility is of greater significance than anything else the music ministers may do.

For choirs and folk groups it means manifesting a mutual respect, a care for one another and a spirit of cooperation. To the extent that jealousy, competition or friction can be discovered, the music group is not fulfilling its most important function to the community.

In determining the location of the choir or group, an image of unity is also to be a factor. Their location should indicate a unity with the entire gathering (GI 257, 274; cf. MCW 38). There are many possibilities but a choir loft no longer recommends itself. Nor do the old sanctuary steps. The old steps may serve as ideal risers, but they immediately divide the assembly into performers and audience. The actual location in any particular church building, of course, should be decided through discussion of the liturgical principle with the music ministers affected.

The cantor or song leader images unity by manifesting a solidarity with the assembly. Righteous attitudes or impressions of superiority from the cantor or song leader detract from the model of unity she or he should be giving:

> The musician belongs first of all to the assembly; he or she is a worshiper above all. Like any member, the pastoral musician needs to be a believer, needs to experience conversion, needs to hear the gospel and so proclaim the praise of God (LMT 64).

LECTORS

Lectors help to build the unified assembly because their ministry is speaking the word of God to us, that word which is a source of our coming together. We have already seen how the summons to become one united people is learned from God's word (Chapter 2). The same word shows us our need for the gift of reconciliation so that we may lay aside the divisions and separations of sinfulness and become one (Chapter 2).

Even though it is the powerful word of God, its effectiveness to some extent is determined by how well the lectors speak it. Lectors have a part to play in whether the word will in fact bring us together.

Three skills especially help the lector to mediate the unifying power of God's word. A lector should be capable of proclamation, be able to communicate with persons, and have the capacity to sustain silence.

Being capable of proclamation means being able to speak with power and presence. It means speaking the words of scripture strongly enough so that they gain the attention of the congregation. Without the strength of proclamation, the hearing of God's word can be lost amid the distractions of life. Then it cannot draw us into the assembly nor can it motivate us to become one reconciled people. A clear, distinct voice with adequate force is the first factor needed for proclamation. Learning to use it well, and practicing the readings faithfully goes without saying. Likewise, mastering microphone technique is also basic.

After a strong voice, demeanor is important. The way we

move and act, what we look like to the congregation, also alerts them to the importance of the word. The basics are standing up straight without swaying or fidgeting, and being deliberate as we approach or leave the lectern.

Besides drawing attention to the word, good demeanor helps in another way to bring us together. It radiates a confidence and firmness about what we are doing, thus giving a certain security to the congregation. More secure in themselves, the congregation is better able to overcome defensive barriers and to realize the unity of faith they have.

The lector in order to be capable of proclamation also must feel a certain urgency about the word of God. Like the prophet Jeremiah, we should be unable to hold back from speaking because the word burns in our bones (Jer 20:7-9). Compulsion is the way St. Paul felt it, with no choice, ruined if he did not hold forth with the word of God (1 Cor 9:16).

Urgent about God's word, the lector should not be asked to handle the announcing chores. A different person is needed to give the opening remarks, indicate the location of hymns, make the necessary parish announcements, etc. Proclamation is a distinct task. It should not be confused with the other speaking parts. The same person attempting both proclamation and announcing weakens and obscures the proclamation. If we could appreciate the awe-filled nature of speaking God's word we would understand how the lector is worn-out and wasted after proclaiming the scriptures. It may be an exaggeration, but, invested fully in God's word, the lector should have energy for nothing else.

The second skill, being able to communicate with other persons, means much more than speaking words in the general vicinity of where these persons are located. Sometimes this seems to be the only thing lectors intend to do. Speaking *to* the congregation rather than *at* the congregation is what communicating means. We have not communicated if we have only formed the air molecules into sound waves and sent them forth.

Communicating involves the listeners as well as the speaker. Lectors, when they read, must be aware that they are telling other persons about the good news. They must be intent on their hearers, reaching out to engage them:

The Lord God has given me
a well trained tongue,
That I might know how to speak to the weary
a word that will rouse them (Is 50:4).

When proclaiming the scriptures it is inadequate to concentrate
only on ourselves, our posture, our delivery skills, etc. We must be
looking to see whether the listeners are indeed hearing, whether
they are understanding, interested and moved by what we are
speaking.

This attentiveness to our listeners is conveyed by eye contact.
From time to time we need to look at the persons to whom we are
reading. Eye contact also helps us to measure our effectiveness. If
we are getting intelligent, comprehending looks in return, then we
know the words are being received and that we are communicating well.

Pausing when competition is too great is another dimension
of good communications. Whenever there is confusion or a
disturbance in the congregation, better to stop. Wait until things
are calmed a bit, then go on. If the congregation is distracted and
not listening to us, no communication is occurring. A favorite
example is the story of one rural church leaving its doors open on
a warm Sunday morning in the spring time. Along came a mama
skunk with her two babies. In they wandered during the liturgy of
the word. The congregation, with gasps and the necessary com-
motion, gave the three a wide berth. The lector, intent on her proclamation, noticed nothing and continued to read through it all.
Her words that morning were not exactly heaven "scent."

Good communications make a particular contribution to the
building of the unified assembly. They create a rapport between
the lector and the congregation. Drawn into a communion with
the lector, the listeners can discover a communion among themselves as well. The common bond of faith being proclaimed
becomes tangible.

It is probably worth grumbling about the missalette from this
perspective of communicating. The missalette hampers communications and thus hinders the efforts of the lector to unify us. It
is very difficult to communicate with another person who is read-

ing something, e.g., the morning newspaper at breakfast. A lector has slim chance if most of the congregation insists on following along in the missalette. Individuals will glean information from the readings, but the communication that unifies us into the gathered assembly will not occur.

Finally, the lector must have the capacity to sustain silence. Before beginning a reading lectors should lead the congregation in a short, silent moment of reflection. Then, upon completion of the reading, they should provide another similar time.

Sustaining silence for the congregation is a very difficult task these days, for we live in the era of the "blaster" and the "boom box." Habits of solitude are not very common. Any time our ears are not filled with sound seems a deprivation. Even a hike into the countryside appears to be pointless if we have not brought along the stereo-walkman.

Still scripture needs silence. Only in silence is scripture appreciated for the mystery it is, God speaking to us. The psalms counsel, "Be still and know that I am God" (46:10, RSV). Zechariah is struck dumb when the angel of God speaks to him telling him he will father John the Baptizer (Lk 1:20). Recorded in the book of Revelation, there is silence for half an hour when the Lamb broke open the seventh seal (8:1). A lector bracketing each reading with an awe-filled silence makes us aware of God's presence in the word.

Alerting us to the mystery of God's presence, the moments of silence provided by the lector contribute to the gathering of the assembly. Our awareness of God's presence always motivates us to unity as we have seen one other time (Chapter 2).

EUCHARISTIC MINISTERS

Eucharistic ministers already have had a turn in our discussions when we considered how the rite of communion builds the unified assembly (Chapter 2). In that discussion the ministers were encouraged to be personally present to the communicants, speaking and listening to them, treating them with simple human dignity. By making the communion moment a greater moment of human communion, the eucharistic ministers in fact provide the better sacramental sign of communion with the Lord. It builds the unified assembly because communion with the Lord is the source of all communion in the eucharistic gathering. Thus the personal presence of the minister to each communicant is of great importance.

There is another dimension of how the care and respect which the minister should show to each communicant builds the unified assembly and brings it to its completion. Much like the ushers, eucharistic ministers help to bond the assembly together by encouraging us to have a caring attitude toward the people with whom we have gathered. Eucharistic ministers who show a respect for and an appreciation of the communicants are examples for us. Seeing their example coaxes us to appreciate the people around us and not to ignore them during the time of communion. The communion moment of course is not the moment for conversation, etc. Still there are the ways we can engage and support each other in the silence appropriate to the moment. The eucharistic ministers should set an atmosphere and mood which helps us to realize these bonds of unity.

Encouraged to be aware of the people with whom we receive communion is a drastic change from some previous forms of eucharistic piety. Yet that earlier discussion of the communion rite (Chapter 2) mentioned how immediate preparations (the Lord's prayer, the sign of peace and the breaking of the bread) (GI 56) called attention to our sisters and brothers gathered with us. Likewise it gave reasons why the thanksgiving after we have received should not be experienced as a time of isolated communion with Jesus alone. Even then we ought to be aware of the persons around us, for communion is complete only when we realize that our bond with the Lord Jesus unites us also with one another.

In fact, since the moment of communion culminates the eucharistic prayer, and the entire celebration (Chapter 3), our coming together in that moment should reach a certain climax and intensity. Here is the full impact of what the ministers of the eucharist are about when they help us to become aware of our communion with each other in the Lord.

This discussion of how eucharistic ministers serve the gathering and help to bring it to its completion, holds a benefit for the ministers themselves. It offers an insight to the question of worthiness which can be especially troubling to lay people when they are asked to be communion ministers. Understandably they hesitate since the blessed sacrament is held in such great reverence and the previous regulation about only the priest's hands touching the host and chalice is still very much remembered.

A sense of serving the community puts the question to rest. We are not asked to be eucharistic ministers because the pastor thinks that our achieved virtue or holiness makes us worthy to handle the blessed sacrament. Rather the community needs our help. Personal piety may recommend us, but service to the community is the reason we are asked.

The "Homely" Side of Eucharist

Special ministers of the eucharist, as lay eucharistic ministers are officially designated, have a special role in bringing God's call of unity—experienced and celebrated in the assembly—to all of humanity and in fact to all of creation. They help to overcome the notion that the eucharist is too holy for daily, human life and for this created world in which we live.

Along the way we began to call holy communion "the bread of angels." In a favorite Latin hymn, *Panis Angelicus,* we sang, "Bread of angels, on thee we feed . . ." It celebrated the holiness of God's presence here on earth in the blessed sacrament. It is a very appropriate sentiment. But unfortunately the piety became exaggerated and the eucharist began to seem far removed from daily life. Day to day living itself was considered more and more as mostly tainted and alien from God. Thus the eucharist appeared to be most fittingly celebrated in a milieu of elaborately vested priests, bejeweled vessels and gold tabernacles. Monks and cloistered sisters removed from the world seemed to be the ones who properly provided the bread and wine.

The celebration of the eucharist should not have an atmosphere so far removed from human living. After all, it involves the very human realities of food and meal. In its origins the eucharist began as common, human gestures of taking, eating and drinking.

According to the Acts of the Apostles the church first celebrated the eucharist in the homes of its members. A pagan writer, in fact, thought the Christians to be atheists because they did not offer sacrifice but ate supper instead. This great holy mystery of the eucharist is very much rooted in human life and belongs to the earth on which we live.

But we had forgotten this "homely" side of the eucharist. We had forgotten that it belongs at home with us, where we live. Figuratively speaking, after the celebration the eucharist should not be left reserved in the tabernacle but taken home.

Lay eucharistic ministers, because they are not professional religion people, help us to recover this side of the eucharist. These lay ministers are the ordinary neighbors and friends. We see them at work, in the supermarket and at the post office. They may distribute holy communion on Sunday, but otherwise their lives are in the world. As a result they help to bridge any exaggerated notions we may have about the eucharist being separated from daily life.

There may be a nostalgia for the eucharist treated only in the fashion of a divine, distant reality. But that was also a "safe" eucharist. The homely eucharist is threatening. It is like having a guest in the guest room. We strive to be on our best behavior. Jesus at home with us means that our brother is close, urging and coaxing us to live as he did. It is easier to live with a divine presence reserved in the tabernacle than it is with Jesus brought home.

There is one more significance to lay people serving as eucharistic ministers. Like lay participation in the eucharistic prayer (Chapter 3), so lay people as eucharistic ministers clearly shows that the entire community celebrates the whole mass. Lay people are not excluded from the more sacred parts. On the other hand, refusing to allow eucharistic ministers to function at all weakens the sign of the entire assembly celebrating.

Currently the regulation remains that lay people may serve as eucharistic ministers only when there is a need and the ordained ministers are too few. However, a request has been made by our bishops to allow lay ministers always to function no matter the number of priests available. According to the request, it would serve as a sign of the diversity of ministries and gifts in the Christian community. From our standpoint it would be a sign of the whole assembly celebrating the entire liturgy. Rome's response was not favorable, but the request has been made.

Do servers help to build the unified assembly in any significant way? The question must be asked because serving has become expendable even though the constitution lists it among the "genuine liturgical ministries" (CSL 29). Some parishes have decided that eliminating all servers is the only just answer to the present discipline which allows only men or boys to serve. Others have dropped the servers because they have had only children serving and the youngsters simply have not been very reliable. Still others, thinking it an appropriate simplification, have the presider himself do all the serving chores.

But any time an active liturgical ministry, especially a lay ministry, like serving, is dropped from the celebration it is a serious matter. It must be given second thoughts, for active ministries incorporate persons to the assembly. Investment is greater when persons are actively involved. There is a greater feeling of belonging and camaraderie when we have specific responsibilities to fulfill for the community.

Dropping the servers eliminates these fundamentals of group building for those who take up this ministry. Thus we do miss an occasion to incorporate some persons to the assembly when servers are not part of the celebration.

Besides the human dynamics of group building, specific aspects of the serving ministry also contribute to our coming together. One of these is the atmosphere of reverence which servers can help to create. In such an atmosphere there is a more tangible experience of our shared faith and of God's presence. Both of these are bonds of unity for us, and we are drawn together by the greater experience of them.

Reverence does require some maturity, though. Servers communicate a sense of love and respect for the celebration by being attentive and involved. Youngsters often become bored, fidget and hardly convey anything positive about the mass occurring in spite of them.

Esteem for the objects handled, the processional cross, the candles, the bread, wine, etc., is another way reverence can be manifested. Holding these objects in full view, as precious gifts or treasures would be held, allows the whole community to experience their spiritual worth.

Deliberate, unhurried movements also help to create the environment of reverence. Moving with grace and ease rather than in a timid, awkward fashion likewise enhances the mood.

There is a lowly side to being a server. Unlike the lectors who proclaim the word of God in their own right, or the eucharistic ministers who distribute the body and blood of the Lord, servers have the mundane, household chores about the altar. Much of their ministry is doing the odds and ends. Moreover they often find themselves doing these things at the biddings of someone else. Previously servers did seem to have a better position in the assembly. They were seated next to the celebrant and appeared to be his special assistants. Now the recommendation is that the presider alone should be prominently seated. Servers should have seats inconspicuously located.

The well-being of every organization requires some members who without regard for position or prestige are willing to do whatever needs doing. The ministry of server should fulfill this function for the Christian community.

But among Christians there is a deeper side to persons who do the lowly tasks in the service of another. They remind us of Jesus' servanthood. Jesus called himself a servant even though people of his time considered it a very disgusting position—much more so than we would. Being the servant, doing the will of another, identifies Jesus. "I have come to do my Father's will" is over and over again on his lips. It is the reason Jesus can reconcile us to God and to one another (Heb 5:7-10). In turn, Jesus makes servanthood the ideal for all of his disciples (Mk 10:42-45; Lk 22:24-27; Jn 13:14). Servers in their ministry of lowly place image this ideal.

Being the image of Jesus the servant strongly recommends

one particular practice currently found in some parishes. It is that of families serving together. Selfless giving and the serving of each other is so necessary to the communion of family life. Thus a family serving together especially mirrors the servanthood of Jesus. The practice may also be an acceptable compromise which—unfortunately at the present—is necessary if women are to have any part in this ministry.

To answer the original question—yes, servers do have some very significant ways in which they help to bring us together. But the reasons for sometimes eliminating servers also represent serious questions. Certainly the ministry does not belong to youngsters. It requires believing adults. Likewise, the exclusion of women cannot continue. There was a stronger defense for it when the server was simply the special assistant to the celebrant. Now the exclusion of women weakens the unified assembly.

PRESIDERS

Although most of us are not ordained and cannot carry out the ministry of presider, still a few remarks about it are in order. The role is that vital to the gathering of the community into a unified assembly. It is essential that all of us understand how the ministry is best exercised.

The way of celebrating the eucharist in the past has had the priest as the center of attention. We saw it in the holy card image of the priest and in the customary designation of the priest alone as the celebrant (Chapter 1). In the general instruction the priest remains a central figure, but not one to be watched from a distance. Now the priest is expected to be in communication with the assembly drawing all of the members into the celebration.

"Within the community of believers . . ." is the way the general instruction begins its description of the priest's role (60). The phrase "invites the people to pray" occurs so frequently that it could be a refrain for the general instruction (32, 47, 53, 56a).

In the section of the instruction entitled "Prayers and Other Parts Assigned to the Priest," details make it clear how the priest is to be attentive to the people. Instructions and introductory remarks made during the celebration are to be adapted to "the concrete situation of the community" (GI 11). Prayers said by the priest should be said in a loud, clear voice if they pertain to the whole assembly (GI 12). Otherwise they should be said "inaudibly" (GI 13).

Once before the importance of the dialogues between the celebrant and the congregation was mentioned (Chapter 2). Actually, as the role of the priest is now described, it is one of constant dialogue with the people. Almost every part of the rite engages the priest directly with the gathered community.

In order to capture the interrelated nature of the role, the general instruction designated the ordained priest as the "presider" (GI 10–13, 60). The designation underlines how the general instruction expands the ministry of the ordained priest so that it incorporates the leading of the assembly.

"Presider," though, has a secular, political sound to it. It can seem to make the ordained priesthood trivial, as though it were just a sociological function in the community. The term presider, however, comes from our tradition. A very early document of the church calls the leader of Sunday worship the "president" (St. Justin, *Apologies*).

The designation presider has one very basic practicality about it. It requires the priest to be aware of the assembly and to manifest that awareness. Speaking the prescribed phrases of the rite with some warmth and expressiveness, as one would speak them to another person, is one of the ways this awareness can be conveyed.

Listening when the responses are made is another. The presider needs to take up a whole stance of listening which includes eye contact, gestures and bodily postures. The entire person of the presider is needed to listen adequately. Fumbling for one's place in the missalette or looking ahead in the sacramentary while the responses are being made betrays a deaf ear.

Some clergy find it difficult to accept this expectation that they should show an awareness of the assembly. Their seminary formation taught them that the mass was carried out solely by their priestly actions. Thus they were to be careful about the rite and attentive to their own inner recollection. Nothing was said about being attentive to the congregation. In fact, the concern was that if a congregation should gather, as on Sunday morning, it would not become a distraction for the priest.

No matter the difficulties, the priest–presider must be alert to the presence of the assembly. It is required so that the celebration will indeed belong to "the people of God arrayed hierarchically" (GI 1), with "the ministers and the faithful" taking "their own proper part . . ." (GI 2; cf. Chapter 3).

BUT ONE MINISTRY

Mentioning the hierarchical nature of the celebration brings up the question of a person doing more than one ministry in the same celebration. It is not recommended. Being hierarchically organized, we are many distinct roles brought together into unity. This is best manifested by several persons each doing a part rather than a few doing everything. The goal is to show forth unity, not simply to get the necessary chores done.

The principle of active participation could also be brought up. Originally the principle was not put forward as a justification for persons doing specific, liturgical ministries. Rather it was the engaging of the whole congregation in the celebration that the principle intended. Still in an accommodated sense the principle applies. Remember its pastoral purpose was to correct the imbalance of the ordained having taken over almost all of the functions in the celebration. So now the principle of active participation cautions us against more than one ministry being done by the same person.

Greater foresight and organizational efforts are needed to involve more persons. It is hardly convenient. But it is the wisdom of the unified assembly that we strive to capture.

HARMONY AMONG MINISTRIES

Harmony is an essential atmosphere which must be found among the liturgical ministers. Only if they show mutual respect and esteem for one another's ministry will their individual efforts be effective in bringing the community together. None should be made to feel inferior.

Lectors must not behave as though the sung psalm response and gospel acclamation were minor interludes between the main events of the word proclaimed. Nor should the musicians tune their instruments during the readings as though it were their break time. The organist ought not to slip out during the homily. (It is more than just a matter of bruising the ego of the homilist.) Ushers dumping together the collection during the eucharistic prayer is one more for the list.

Liturgical ministers can give the impression that they are bit actors relaxing off-stage until they receive the cue to deliver their few lines. A better image is that of the coach and waiting players who follow the developments of the game and urge on the ones playing. Liturgical ministers ought to show that kind of support for each other. The congregation can then follow this example of enthusiastic harmony, and together with them become the unified assembly.

Urging liturgical ministers to manifest a unity among themselves begins with St. Paul. His reasons go far beyond those of being the good example for the community. Bonds of faith motivate his earnest request. "There are different kinds of spiritual gifts but the same Spirit; there are different forms of service but the same Lord" (1 Cor 12:5). We recognize in these words Paul's anxiety for the whole of the Corinthian community, that they would manifest their unity in faith. St. Paul always was intent that Christians should not miss a chance to show their bonds of union. Behind our efforts at being in accord with the other ministries as we carry out our own is Paul's overarching insistence for all Christians when they are together: ". . . complete my joy by being of the same mind, with the same love, united in heart, thinking one thing" (Phil 2:2).

5.

Gathering Together:
All of Humanity, All of Creation

With all this talk about building the unified assembly, it might seem that a successful celebration would be one which everyone enjoys and no one wants to leave. We might recall how after the transfiguration, St. Peter exclaimed to Jesus, "It is good for us to be here. Let us pitch our tents and stay" (cf. Mk 9:1–8). When we work so hard at the things that promise to change our congregations into gathered communities, things like vigorous music, strong responses, hospitality, etc., it is no wonder if our vision of success is people seated together, participating enthusiastically and no one leaving early.

But success is something else. The *Constitution on the Sacred Liturgy*, in fact the entire Second Vatican Council, had as its goal, "to strengthen those aspects of the Church which can help summon all of mankind [sic] into her embrace" (#1). The liturgy in particular ". . . reveals the Church as a sign raised above the nations" (CSL 2). Under this sign the scattered people of God "are being gathered into one until there is one fold and one shepherd" (CSL 2).

Here is the greater goal of our efforts at building the unified assembly. They are part of the council's concern for the church as God's instrument calling all of humanity into one. They are practical ways in which the church celebrating the liturgy can become the sign about which the council speaks.

Thus, building the unified assembly has a purpose beyond itself. It is to make known God's will that all may be one (Jn 17:21).

As we celebrate the eucharist we pray: "In mercy and love unite all your children wherever they may be" (Eucharistic Prayer III).

The greater goal brings a new dimension to those two basic insights behind the priority of gathering together. It shows us why the church is essentially a community, a united body of people, and why the celebration of the eucharist needs to reflect this aspect of the church. Celebrating the liturgy as a gathered assembly, we become a tiny realization of God's intent for the coming together of all humanity.

Another essential quality of the church was reemphasized by the council. It is the mission of the church to the world. In its opening description, the council named the church "the light of all nations" (DCC 1). It spoke of the "encompassing mission of the Church" and the "urgency to the Church's task of bringing all men [sic] to full union with Christ" (DCC 1).

Celebrating the liturgy so that we become a unified assembly is not only a realization of the church as a community but also a way for the church to accomplish its mission. The unity we manage to have in our liturgical gathering shows others God's plan for the unity of all persons. In gathering together to celebrate the liturgy, the church becomes a means for others to learn of God's will. Or in the words of the council, the church becomes a sign gathering all humanity into one.

There is an immediate insight to be gained from the church accomplishing its mission through the celebration of the eucharist. The unified assembly intended as a sign of the church should always have its "full complement of God's holy people" (CSL 41). It must never resemble a little, exclusive, "in" community.

No doubt one of our greatest difficulties is getting people to recognize each other's existence and to pay some attention to one another. The bonds of faith that unite us must be appreciated and experienced. Still it must remain clear that our intent is not a cozy friendship of like-minded persons enjoying each other's company. The plan of God incorporates everyone. Jesus' parable of the wedding feast is the example. People are summoned from the streets and alleys, the highways and hedgerows so that the banquet hall will be full (Lk 14:21, 23).

Our eucharistic table best manifests God's plan when there is no exclusivity among the disciples who gather about it. We form the unified assembly when bankers, street people, the shaggy-headed and the well-groomed are all drawn together. The unity we manifest in our eucharistic assembly has another dimension to its goal. God's will for union not only seeks to bring all of humanity into one but also extends to the whole of creation:

> . . . the mystery of his will . . . as a plan for the fullness of time, to sum up all things in Christ, in heaven and on earth (Eph 1:9–10).

The purpose of our coming together for the liturgy incorporates this part of God's intent as well.

God bringing together all of creation through Jesus is a theme repeatedly found in the mass prayers. "He has come to lift all things to himself, to restore unity to creation" (Christmas Preface II). "The joy of the resurrection renews the whole world" (closing line of the Prefaces from Easter to Pentecost). Creation, for its part, is to unite in a song of praise to God. "Earth unites with heaven to sing the new song of creation" (Preface, Fourth Sunday of Lent, also Preface, Holy Eucharist II); "all creation rightly gives you praise" (Eucharistic Prayer III). Our task is to lead this one prayer in praise of God, "in the name of every creature under heaven, we too praise your glory" (Preface of Eucharistic Prayer IV; cf. Preface, Sundays in Ordinary Time V).

Leading creation's one song to the glory of God requires us to show unity among ourselves. Separate, disparate voices cannot lead the song with any honesty. Gathering together for the eucharist provides the occasion when we show some unity among ourselves, and hence can bring all creation into a singular hymn. Thus our unified assembly, built as we celebrate, helps to make known the unity God wills for the whole universe.

Once more an event in the life of St. Peter can provide some insight for us. From his Jewish background Peter would have considered some of creation to be unclean or impure, that is, unfit to be part of any worship of God. He is given a vision in which he

sees a great canvas lowered from heaven. It contained every creature of the earth. Peter is told they are all holy and belong to God.
He should not hold himself aloof from any of them (Acts 10:9–18).

The episode prepares Peter to accept Gentiles into the
church. Until that time the church had been made up entirely of
Jewish members. Gentiles were considered unclean, and hence,
unacceptable—so it was thought (Acts 11:1–3, 17). As Peter's eyes
were opened to a greater horizon, so our eyes are opened. God
embraces all things and everyone. In building the unified assembly, we are to summon all humanity and creation into God's
communion.

If, in fact, the little things we do in building the eucharistic
assembly are to accomplish such a magnificent purpose, then
there needs to be a sending forth. We must leave the assembly to
tell others what we have glimpsed and experienced. What begins
in our celebration is to flow forth into all of life.

It was necessary to come together. There we discovered our
faith was shared. It was strengthened in that experience. Our confidence also was bolstered by knowing the security of belonging.
We discovered that we were part of a community which accepted
us and cared for us. We have also learned our greater mission, the
calling of all humanity into union and the joining together of all
creation in praise of God's name (cf. Eucharistic Prayer III).
Worshiping privately we would not have grasped so well this
great mission, nor would we have the same strength and confidence with which to take it up.

But now the dismissal. It is brief but insistent. The general
instruction simply says we are sent "back to doing good works,
while praising and blessing the Lord" (#57). The actual words of
the dismissal, "Go in the peace of Christ," and its variations, do not
capture the strength of the moment. It is much more: "Go! You are
sent!" The dismissal should forcefully thrust us into the world to
make known what we have learned about God's plan and to lead
the one great shout of praise and thanksgiving:

"... in the unity of the Holy Spirit, all glory and honor is
yours, almighty Father, for ever and ever" (Doxology).

While the words of the whole dismissal may need greater strength, the bidding, "Go in peace," has its own power in sending us forth to our task. It is not at all a farewell wish intended only for ourselves, even though it may sound that way: "[Jesus] said to them again, 'Peace be with you. As the Father has sent me, so I send you'" (Jn 20:21).

Throughout the mass, whenever we have prayed for peace it has been for the world. Very clearly in the third eucharistic prayer we pray, ". . . advance the peace and salvation of all the world." The petition from the prayer embellishing the Our Father, "grant us peace in our day," is a petition for a peaceful world in which to live, as well as for personal, interior peace. The prayer from the rite of peace prays for the "peace and unity" of God's kingdom. Remember, God's kingdom is to be a harmony among all of creation.

"Grant us peace," the ending petition of the Lamb of God, also is for the world. It accompanies the breaking of the bread, a sign of Christ's death, the source of unity that is to draw all persons into one: ". . . Jesus was going to die for the nation, and not only for the nation, but also to gather into one the dispersed children of God" (Jn 11:51–52; cf. Jn 12:32, Eph 2:14–18, Rv 5:9). "Go in peace," coming at the end, voices once more our insistent prayer for peace in the world.

As part of the dismissal these words send us forth bearing the peace of Christ. That for which we have prayed is now ours to give. "Go in peace" commissions us to become a source of peace for the world.

Gathering together into the unified assembly has had its part to play in preparing us to be that source of peace. During the celebration our prayers for peace and unity in the world begin with the peace we ourselves have received from Christ. Having his peace we pray for the world:

Lord, may this sacrifice
which has made our peace with you,
advance the peace and salvation of all the world
(Eucharistic Prayer III).

Gathered together in Christ's peace for this celebration, we come to know ourselves as the "family." It motivates us to seek Christ's gift of peace and unity for everyone:

> Father, hear the prayers of the family
>   you have gathered here before you.
> In mercy and love unite all your children
>   wherever they may be (Eucharistic Prayer III).

By this time we realize that prayers about Christ's peace among us, our being gathered together and our being family should not remain sentiments expressed only in words. There should also be some experience of them in the celebration. All along it has been the reason we try to become the unified assembly as we celebrate. Thus the strength of these prayers for unity and peace depends upon our efforts at gathering together. We become a source of peace for the world by trying to be the unified assembly.

Indeed the building of the unified assembly has not been for its own sake. During the time of the assembly we worked to realize an experience of the faith bonds that join us together. In that experience we have come to know Christ's gift of himself which unites us with our sisters and brothers, and the whole of humanity. We have also gained the vision of all creation becoming one before God.

As the assembly comes to a conclusion we are dismissed to a new work, building the peace and harmony of all creation. Our bonds of unity must now reach to the entire world. Christ's peace is to ripple out from us to the whole universe. "The gift you have received, give as a gift" (Mt 10:8).